Leonarde's Ghost

Habent sua fata libelli

Leonarde's Ghost

Popular Piety and
"The Appearance of a Spirit"
in 1628

Translated with
Introduction & Annotations

Kathryn A. Edwards
Susie Speakman Sutch

Sixteenth Century Essays & Studies 82
Truman State University Press

Cover art: Anonymous. "Murder Reveng'd: or, God's Judgment on the Bloody
Father." 17th century English broadsheet. Beinecke Rare Book and Manuscript
Library, Yale University.

"Histoire de l'apparition d'un esprit arrive dans la ville de Dole, le 24 juillet 1628,"
by Albert de Saint-Jacques (also known as Christophe Mercier).

Cover design: Teresa Wheeler
Type: Minion Pro © Adobe Systems Inc., Raphael © Adobe Systems Inc., and
    Adobe Wood Type Ornaments Two © Adobe Systems Inc.
Printed by: Thomson-Shore, Dexter, Michigan USA

Library of Congress Cataloging-in-Publication Data
Mercier, Christophe, 17th cent.
    [Histoire de l'apparition d'un esprit arrive dans la ville de Dole le 24 juillet 1628.
English]
    Leonarde's ghost : popular piety and "the appearance of a spirit" in 1628 / trans-
lated with an introduction and annotations by Kathryn A. Edwards and Susie
Speakman Sutch.
        p. cm. — (Sixteenth century essays & studies ; v. 82)
    Includes bibliographical references and index.
    ISBN 978-1-931112-79-6 (pbk. : alk. paper)
    1. Ghosts—France—Dole. 2. Colin, Leonarde, 17th cent. (Spirit) 3. Roy,
Huguette, 17th cent. I. Edwards, Kathryn A., 1964– II. Sutch, Susie Speakman.
III. Title.
    BF1472.F8M4713 2008
    133.1'294447—dc22

                                                                    2008003992

The paper in this publication meets or exceeds the minimum requirements of the
American National Standard for Information Sciences—Permanence of Paper for
Printed Library Materials, ANSI Z39.48–1992.

Contents

History of the Appearance of a Spirit
Which Happened in the City of Dole,
July 24, 1628

Acknowledgments

Although we, the editors and translators, have benefited from community enthusiasm to an extent that our story's protagonists would have envied, the process of producing this work has taken far longer than any of the characters in it might have expected. The accumulated debts reflect that process.

We would like to thank Mlle. Danielle Ducout, past director of Dole's municipal library, and her staff for their assistance in checking Dusilet's copy of Mercier's manuscript, providing microfilms, and finding other contemporary materials. The municipal archive was equally helpful, providing volumes of materials on short order. This project has also benefited from the support of various North American institutions. The History Department of the University of Southern Mississippi generously granted a year's leave, which was spent at the University of Utah as an Eccles Research Fellow of the Tanner Humanities Center where this translation was begun, while the Folger Shakespeare Library provided a congenial and stimulating setting to complete this book and begin more comprehensive research on early modern ghosts and apparitions. The National Endowment of the Humanities, American Historical Association, Fulbright-Hayes Commission, Institut Français de Washington, and the University of South Carolina all provided additional funds for research in Dole, Belgium, and the Franche-Comté.

Students at the University of Southern Mississippi, Utah State University, and University of South Carolina enthusiastically acted as test audiences for various drafts of this manuscript, and we have tried to incorporate their comments, concerns, and questions. Various individuals have also taken time from their busy schedules to make suggestions about the drafts and translation strategies; we are especially grateful for the help of Jim Bono, Robyn Curtis, Iréne d'Alméida, Carlos Eire, Marc Elliott, Jennifer Hammond, Norm Jones, Eric Midelfort, and Elizabeth Peterson. Discussions with many scholars have strengthened both the introduction and translation in ways of which they are probably unaware but for which we are exceeding grateful. We would like to thank Anston Bosman, Tom Brady, Gene Brucker, Edmund Campos, Roger Chartier, Alix Cooper, Johannes Dillinger, Sarah Ferber, Kasey Grier, Mack Holt, Birgit Houben, Paul Johnson, Rebecca Laroche, Tom Lekan, David Lederer, Peter Marshall, John O'Malley, Pat Parker, Tim Raylor, Fred Schurink, Anne Jacobson Schutte, Bill Sherman, Peter Stallybrass, Randy Starn, Michael Steppat, Michael Wolfe, and especially, Anne-Laure Van Bruaene. David Whitford generously read several drafts, and the manuscript is much the better for it. Bill Bouwsma and Robert Brentano would have thoroughly enjoyed Huguette's story, and it is our loss that we cannot share it with them.

Finally, it is difficult to express our gratitude to and thankfulness for our colleagues, Laura V. Truffaut and Kenneth R. Berri, for their unflagging interest in this project. They helped to verify the transcription of the French manuscript, provided numerous linguistic refinements to the translation, and made valuable suggestions for the introduction. Without their aid, Huguette's, Leonarde's, and Christophe's voices would not come through as clearly as they do.

Foreword

The Editorial Process

The manuscript containing Huguette's story is housed today in Dole's main municipal library. It remains largely unknown, its binding giving no sense of its contents. A small book, it is sandwiched between large legal tomes from the early modern period. A brief note in the Dole library catalog lists the manuscript as "The History of the Appearance of a Spirit Which Happened in the City of Dole" and dates it to the early eighteenth century, despite repeated textual and material evidence that places the manuscript several decades earlier. While other contemporary printed books and bound manuscripts merited further description in the same catalog, no such detail is provided for Huguette's story. The inside of the front cover (the pastedown) attributes "The History" to Christophe Mercier, who was more commonly known by the name he took when professing as a Discalced Carmelite, Albert de St. Jacques. Mercier's voice is clearly discernible in the story as he comments on events he narrates and at times speaks directly to the reader. According to this same note, the surviving manuscript is itself not the original but a copy of Mercier's original manuscript. This copy was made later in the seventeenth century by Leonel Dusilet, dean of Neublans and member of Dole's college of canons. But the manuscript's mysteries do not end there. Within "The History," there are repeated references to what "I" saw, what "I" felt, and what "I" believed. The "I" belongs to a third author peeking out from the manuscript, namely, Huguette Roy herself.

These intricacies were among the many aspects of Huguette's story that intrigued us as editors and translators. Aside from the insights the manuscript gives into early modern society, as outlined at the beginning of this book's introduction, "The History of the Appearance of a Spirit" is also a fascinating study of the ways people wrote who are not part of the canon of literary greats more commonly taught. The manuscript's French is rough and the author makes grammatical mistakes, but his style of writing, its tone, and even its flaws are consummately those of an author with middling abilities from the early modern Franche-Comté. In other words, whether the author was Mercier or Dusilet, he wrote in a style shared by many more people from his time than the literary luminaries so often presented as representative. Given that the manuscript combined these qualities with those of an appealing and illuminating story, we believed it would be ideal to present to both a general audience and readers with more specialized interests.

We were also convinced that the original story and the ways of thinking conveyed and formed by language could here best be appreciated through a translation that presented them as close to their original style, grammar, and pace as possible. By providing modern readers with a text that preserves much of the vitality and, at times, unevenness of the original French, we hope to impart some glimmer of what it was like to speak and think like a person from the Franche-Comté in the seventeenth century, to reinforce that sense of familiarity and difference that often attracts people to the study of history. Because we approached the text with such distinct editorial ideas in mind, we have provided here a sketch of the decisions they led us to make when translating and editing this manuscript.[1]

When preparing "The History" for publication, we were presented with many of the same circumstances faced by anyone working with early modern French texts and, in some cases, early modern texts more generally. By and large the manuscript is written in relatively clear, educated handwriting, but certain misreadings or mistranscriptions of Mercier's original have crept in and have required correction.[2] As was typical in the period, the spelling of proper names and uncommon words is phonetic, which means that one person's name may be spelled differently in differ-

---

[1]For more technical details about how the manuscript was edited and translated, see "Notes on Translation" available at http://tsup.truman.edu. Also available on this website is our French-language transcription of "The History" with footnotes clarifying specific editorial decisions.

[2]Delsalle, *Lexique pour l'étude de la Franche-Comté à l'époque des Habsbourg*; and Duchet-Suchaux and Duchet-Suchaux, *Dictionnaire du français régional de Franche-Comté*.

ent parts of the text. Huguette's neighbor Jeanne Massey had her last name written three ways. Huguette's own last name, "Roy," also appears as "Roye," and it is almost impossible to decide exactly how many *s*'s belong in the name of Jacques Deniset, one of Huguette's hosts while she was on pilgrimage. Since French punctuation did not yet follow set rules, sentences within the original text appear extraordinarily long and complex; at times a reader has to wonder if the speakers ever paused for breath. Personal pronouns, too, are used inconsistently when referring to the spirit: is it a she, a he, or an it? Sudden shifts in verb tenses, the complete omission of the subject pronoun where modern French requires one, and the disagreement of subject and verb or the gender of adjectives with the nouns that they modify are all among the many incongruities the manuscript presents to a reader, although these complexities are not unique to it, as any reader of early modern French legal or ecclesiastical records can attest.

In addition to the usual complications that arise because of linguistic differences between French and English, we were also faced with translation decisions that could affect the fundamental meaning of the text in unusual ways. In "The History," the ghost takes almost a month—that is, half the manuscript—to reveal its spiritual status, and the extent to which the spirit is human is fundamental in determining its legitimacy and Huguette's orthodoxy. As such, it matters whether the author believes the spirit to be male (he), female (she), or neuter (it). Our author treats the spirit's gender in such a way as to reinforce its orthodoxy while retaining the narrative drama of the story. In English, where the words for ghost and spirit have no gender, that aspect of the story's construction can easily be lost.

As the above example of gendering a ghost suggests, our author also had more idiosyncratic concerns, and these peculiarities are reflected in his writing. For instance, he uses Latin language structures that can make his meaning difficult to grasp, and he is often mistaken when he quotes or paraphrases Latin texts. He repeatedly changes voice in the narration—from "I" to "we" and again to the third person, all in the same paragraph—a practice that could indicate either undisciplined or uneducated writing or as is more likely, given Mercier's and Dusilet's background, an extremely close identification with the people and events presented in "The History." The vividness of the author's experience is reflected in the vividness of his language. He presents characters as having real personalities and depicts emotional states such as reverence, awe, cynicism, anger, and frustration in dialogue and description as befits not merely the experiences they are undergoing, but their social and educational level as well. These qualities do not prevent and may even have fostered the development of textual inaccuracies. He misidentifies regional cults of the Virgin Mary and the locations of distant villages. Mercier also has difficulties keeping track of the apparition's schedule. In chapter 1, he notes that the spirit arrived at different times each day, while in chapter 3 he mentions that the spirit's hour "is approaching," implying that it followed a predictable schedule. Repeating the same pattern, in chapter 11 Mercier writes about the spirit's regular twice-a-day visits, whereas earlier in the text the spirit has only been appearing once a day.

Given the challenges these inconsistencies posed and our reasons for presenting "The History" to a modern, English-language audience, our translation enterprise has been governed by two seemingly contradictory principles: clarity of the English text and fidelity to the French original. Yet these two fundamentals were not as mutually exclusive as they may seem. Throughout our translation, we have endeavored to produce an English text that is intelligible while remaining faithful to the seventeenth-century French of the original. Where these two principles collided, we chose to focus on clarity. We have also tried, as far as possible, to preserve the liveliness and spontaneity of the original French by respecting its syntax, inconsistencies of verb tense, and tendency to structure sentences out of strings of participial phrases and clauses. We have attempted to keep punctuation to a minimum, as in the original French text, but have added it when necessary to promote readability and clarity.

When dealing with a manuscript copy, editors are bound to come across misreadings and mistranscriptions. "The History" is no exception. Where we have discerned a blatant misreading, lapse, or mistranscription in the manuscript Dusilet produced, the demands of clarity have again prevailed. In such cases, and they are minimal, we have relied on our correction when we translated the text into English rather than introduce more confusion by retaining Dusilet's misreading and correcting it in footnotes to the translation. We also have made some clarifications to the original pronouns or nouns, most commonly adding a proper noun or a verb. We have cut some of the use of the conjunction "and" in favor of briefer and more intelligible sentences, and on very rare occasions we have converted a string of participial clauses into independent clauses. Finally, we have introduced contractions into certain segments of dialogue in order to approximate the liveliness of direct speech. Huguette and Leonarde argue with the speed and slurring common in family quarrels, and their dialogue should reflect their passion.

Despite our best efforts, there remain elements that will be jarring to the English reader: the ambiguous personal references, the mountains of adverbs and adjectives, the use of past and future tenses to describe the same events, and the sentences that can extend for several manuscript pages. By minimizing new punctuation, insertion of words and phrases, and division of sentences except when absolutely necessary for clarity, we have presented a language that can seem quite odd at times to a modern English reader, such as the enormous sentence at the end of chapter 13. Such sentences, though, also give a modern audience a more immediate sense of how the manuscript actually reads and the way readers over the centuries could draw diverse conclusions from, in part, this linguistic imprecision. It is a vagueness that Mercier, Huguette, and Leonarde could exploit. For similar reasons, we have also avoided regularizing verb tenses, which can make following the story somewhat exciting as Mercier switches tenses with abandon. The translation's roughness reflects the roughness, vitality, rhythms, and ambiguities of the original manuscript, further illustrating the complexities in any language's evolution. For us, the "ugliness" of Mercier's French, to paraphrase a frequent complaint we made at the beginning of the project, has become yet another way "The History" offers insight into ugliness and beauty, the mundane and the wonderful in the lives of early modern Europeans.

Introduction

A Setting for a Ghost Story

 On 7 April 1628, a spirit visited a poor, pregnant woman in the city of Dole, the capital of the Franche-Comté, a province in the far west of the Holy Roman Empire. This apparition was dressed in white but appeared to be a young chambermaid, someone the woman could ill afford to hire. For over fifty days, it spoke to the woman, cared for her and her newborn son, and demonstrated its good nature to almost everyone it encountered. Although the spirit came to aid Huguette Roy, the young mother, over time it revealed that it too needed help. It was a suffering soul desperate to escape purgatory. Many people in Dole were both curious about and frightened of the ghost. A young man named Christophe Mercier left a record of their experiences, including the impressions he gained from being in the room with the spirit. When Mercier wrote the history of Huguette Roy and the spirit who visited her, Leonarde Colin, he may have seen his work as having many purposes: to glorify God, to teach orthodox piety, and to exonerate both Huguette and Leonarde, among others. Although his success in most of these goals remains unknowable, he apparently accomplished the latter. Huguette was never prosecuted or even roughly questioned, unlike so many women in the early seventeenth century who claimed to see or hear spirits.

If, however, he intended to establish a cult around Leonarde or glorify the town in which a blessed soul appeared, he was less successful. The original manuscript has disappeared, and the town council's minutes and the records of the region's religious houses make no mention of Huguette

1

or Leonarde after the time of this story. There are no relics, no pious broadsheets, and no devotions. Although Mercier's manuscript was copied, bound in leather, and eventually placed in Dole's burgeoning municipal library, their story seems to have merited no more than an antiquarian's interest. In the studies of local piety during the seventeenth century scattered throughout regional journals, they are only mentioned sporadically, as a historical oddity. Their most recent claim to fame was a brief article during the 1980s in the local paper, *Les Dépêches*, although the picture of the building in which Huguette lived and which has survived, albeit highly renovated, took as much space as the copy itself.

Despite this neglect, Huguette and Leonarde's story has much to offer. Mercier's account provides an approachable entrance into a region rarely treated in English-language histories, even though the kings of France and the Holy Roman emperors felt it was important enough to fight over it for centuries. More importantly, however, it opens a rare window into the spirituality, piety, and daily lives of "ordinary" people in early modern Europe. While it does so through an extraordinary event—a ghostly apparition—it also emphasizes the mundane: the furniture in Huguette's home, connections within her neighborhood, and relationships between family members. Mercier's sympathy for Huguette molds his account, but her story avoids the constraints of accounts discovered in legal archives; Huguette is never directly placed in a situation where she is fighting for her life, and legal process does not direct those observing or questioning her. Given the timing of Leonarde's appearance, "The History" also testifies to the promotion and practice of Catholic reform in a region that had, increasingly during the sixteenth and seventeenth centuries, come to define itself through its Catholicism. Huguette and Leonarde's history is thus a story integrating housework and holiness, gossip and theology, friendship and penance, centered around a young woman and a ghost on a social and spiritual journey. Huguette, Leonarde, Christophe, and their community experienced an extraordinary event, but it also was one to be expected and, if divinely instituted, embraced in early modern Catholicism.

In order to understand this mix of the ordinary and extraordinary, it is necessary to understand the setting of the story: the free county (Franche-Comté) of Burgundy and, in particular, the county's capital, Dole, where Huguette lived and the story's events occurred. Much of this town and region's history is available only in French, so much of the local context may be unfamiliar to many readers. Rather than providing an introduction that neatly integrates Huguette's haunting into the society of the early modern France-Comté, we have separated the original source and the historical context. This division allows readers to focus more readily on specific topics in the introduction, using the information as a foundation for their own analysis without being told how to interpret the text. We hope that our way of organizing the information will permit readers to draw independent conclusions using varied techniques of historical and literary analysis and to appreciate more immediately the fear associated with the appearance of a ghost and the wonder of this early modern ghost story.

CHARACTERS IN THE STORY

Some of the people and events in this manuscript can be found in other contemporary records. Huguette Roy and her husband, Antoine Roget, lived in Dole during the first half of the seventeenth century. They had a total of five children: two girls and three boys. The birth of the middle child, Claude, prompted the haunting, and his record in the baptismal register corresponds to the date provided by Mercier.[1] In addition, a month after Leonarde's first apparition, the Dole town council sent two members of the council to check on the disturbances occurring on the street where Huguette lived. There are no accounts of urban unrest during May 1628; thus it is plausible that their visit was because of Leonarde's apparitions, which were attracting quite a crowd by that stage.

There are also supporting documents from the decades following the haunting. A Claude Roget survived childhood and lived in Dole during the mid-seventeenth century. He may have even joined the Discalced Carmelite friars, one of the reformed religious orders for which Mercier suggests Claude will have a special affinity. Evidence of Claude's extraordinary infancy is corroborated in a letter from 1641 by Jean Boyvin, mayor of Dole and member of the city's chief legal body, the Parlement, to a colleague and

---

[1] Archives municipales de Dole [hereafter AMDole], GG12, fol. 218. Before Claude's birth, they had two daughters, Carola and Marguerita, baptized on 25 July 1625 and 3 April 1627, respectively; AMDole, GG9. After Claude's birth, they would have two more sons: Antoine, who was baptized on 1 November 1630, and Nicolas, who was baptized on 8 Oct. 1634; AMDole, GG15, fols. 83r & 185v. As was customary in this era, both of the sons had godparents of a higher social status than those of the daughters. Unfortunately the other baptismal and death registers were only kept sporadically in Dole for the first half of the seventeenth century, so we cannot confirm any additional births or deaths.

friend, Jean-Jacques Chifflet, living in the town of Besançon, located approximately thirty miles northeast of Dole. In this letter, Boyvin provides a summary whose outlines are essentially identical to those given in Mercier's account: a spirit troubled a young and naive woman, this spirit was eventually revealed to be a suffering soul, and the young woman and community rallied to provide what was necessary for the soul to ascend to heaven.[2] According to the letter, Boyvin gained his information directly from Father Orlando, a Jesuit at Dole, who was one of the Jesuits who helped guide Huguette and test the spirit; while none of the Jesuits' names is given in the text translated here, a Father Orlando was among Dole's Jesuits in the first half of the seventeenth century. Boyvin also delivers the sad news that Huguette died sometime before 1641 in one of the outbreaks of plague that swept through the Franche-Comté.

There are two other characters who are central to Huguette's story and for whom contemporary information exists: the text's authors, Christophe Mercier and Leonel Dusilet. Huguette, the woman who saw the spirit, did not herself compose the text translated here; if she had, it would be an even more extraordinary document than it is. Instead, the only surviving manuscript is attributed to Christophe Mercier, who implies that he was Huguette's confessor, although he may only be one of the many clergy observing events in Huguette's rooms. Mercier was a young man, probably in his twenties, at the time of the events recounted here, but he remained committed to visionary piety and to writing books throughout his life. In 1664 he composed a book in praise of the contemplative life called *La Sainte Solitude* (Holy Solitude), which also showed his awareness of Catholic reform movements in the Low Countries. In 1673 he wrote *La vie de la venerable mère Térèse de Iesus fondatrice des Carmelites de la Franche-Comté de Bourgogne* (The Life of the Venerable Mother Theresa of Jesus, founder of the Carmelites of the Franche-Comté of Burgundy); two years later he published a French translation of a Spanish book listing the visions of purgatorial souls experienced by a Discalced Carmelite sister.[3] Each of these works marks him as a participant in the sixteenth- and seventeenth-century Catholic reformed movements epitomized in the lives of Saints Teresa of Avila and John of the Cross. Claude, in fact, joined the Discalced Carmelites, took the name of Albert de St. Jacques, and became the head

---

[2] Bibliothèque municipale de Besançon [hereafter BMB], Collection Chifflet, ms. 103, 3 June 1641, fols. 146r–47r.

[3] Albert de St. Jacques, trans., *Lumiere aux vivans par l'experience des morts.*

(provincial) of the Burgundian province of that order. As such, he administered communities of Discalced Carmelites throughout the Franche-Comté; as a Discalced Carmelite himself, he presumably practiced the intense, contemplative, and somewhat reclusive piety for which the male branch was known. As the provincial, it is also likely that he traveled to the Low Countries and possibly even Spain or Italy for meetings. Certainly he participated in theological and literary exchanges between those regions. While there is no evidence that he attended the university at Dole, it is highly unlikely that someone attaining his prominence in the Discalced Carmelite friars would have had no advanced education, and his writings testify to some specialized theological training. The remaining records for the Franche-Comté's Discalced Carmelite friars are quite sparse, so nothing is known about his other activities. Although there is no surviving contemporary record of his death, eighteenth-century accounts note Albert de St. Jacques as having died in 1680.

The extant manuscript about Huguette's haunting was, however, copied by someone else, albeit someone who may have been well acquainted with Mercier. According to a short note on its inside front cover, "The History" that has come down to us is a copy of Mercier's original manuscript made by Leonel Dusilet, dean of Neublans and member of Dole's college of canons. Dole's registers attest to the activities of a Leonard Dusilet in the late seventeenth century, and given the family's genealogy, the linguistic similarities of the names, and the concurrence between the dating of the manuscript and Leonard's clerical activities, it is likely that Leonard and Leonel are the same man. Leonard himself may have experienced the events Mercier described; he died in late 1697 at the venerable age of eighty-eight.[4] As dean of Neublans, Dusilet was a member of the religious community in Dole charged with ministering to the city's residents, the college of canons attached to Our Lady (Notre Dame) of Dole. It appears that Dusilet lived in Dole, unlike some of the other canons, and so may even have known Mercier. Records of the college attest that he regularly attended meetings of that community in the second half of the seventeenth century, although he stopped coming several years before his death.[5] Although the Dusilet family would gain some regional prominence in the

---

[4]AMDole, GG54, fol. 5r. The chances that Dusilet was the author of this story are, however, slight. A comparison of linguistic structures between this manuscript and those books composed by Albert de St. Jacques shows striking similarities in syntax, vocabulary, and tone.

[5]Archives départementales du Jura [hereafter ADJ], G96.

eighteenth century, in the seventeenth it still only enjoyed middling status—enough to have a son appointed a canon but not enough for richer appointments or further clerical advancement. As with Mercier, however, little remains to trace Dusilet's career and even less exists to assess his beliefs. Because of these circumstances, the "history" Mercier and Dusilet have prepared is not only the best account of the lives of Huguette, her family, and friends, but it is the best testament available of the spiritual commitments and concerns of two prominent clerics in the Franche-Comté during the height of its Catholic reform.

HUGUETTE'S HOME: THE CITY OF DOLE AND ITS REGION

Nestled in the rolling foothills that mark the beginning of the Jura mountains, Dole in the early twenty-first century is a market town, local administrative seat, and popular vacation spot for those seeking peace and quiet. To the west lie the flat, fertile plains of the Côte d'Or (the gold coast) with its fields of wheat and mustard; its prosperous villages testify to the appropriateness of its name. To the east of Dole the foothills build, eventually becoming the fortified peaks and rocky gorges that separate the county of Burgundy (Franche-Comté), to which Dole belongs, from the Swiss Confederation. From all directions, small hamlets and farming villages mark the approach to Dole, and it is often difficult to tell where these communities end and the suburbs of Dole begin. On the city's periphery and in neighboring villages, horses graze and gardens thrive in the large backyards that give the area a decidedly rural flavor. To the south of Dole, however, the river Doubs provides a striking division between these rural suburbs and the city itself. Bordered by the river and roads built where the city's walls once stood, the center of Dole retains its early modern character and only takes about fifteen minutes to walk across. Most of its buildings date from the sixteenth through the eighteenth centuries, and the winding streets they line make driving anything other than a compact car a challenge. The church of Our Lady dominates Dole's skyline, and on Saturday mornings the square in front of it hosts an open-air market that overflows onto the neighboring streets and sidewalks. Religious houses, such as those of the Jesuits and Franciscans, are located in this center as well and reflect the same aesthetic tastes as the many prosperous town houses on the major thoroughfares. Dole's organization and architecture, as well as road names such as rue du Gouvernement (Government Street),

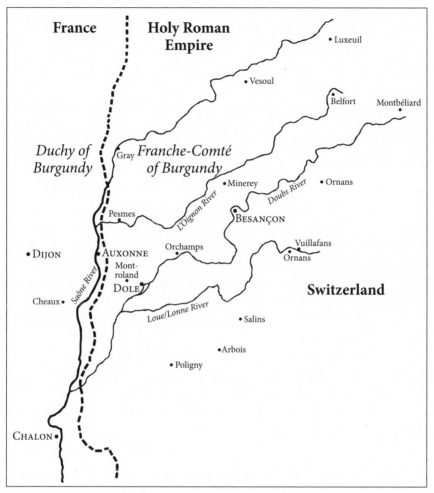

The Dole Region and Key Cities of the Franche-Comté. Map by Kathryn A. Edwards.

bear witness to its historical stature.

Much of this now picturesque landscape had just been or was being constructed at the time of the story translated here (1628) and represents a rebuilding and expansion of Dole's previous infrastructure after more than a century's turmoil.[6] This history, particularly the repeated threats Dole faced from France and challenges to the oligarchy's authority by rival town councils, remained immediate to Dole's secular and ecclesiastical leaders.

[6]The most recent synthesis of the county's history is Walter, *Histoire de la Franche-Comté*.

When these individuals experienced or heard of apparitions and visionaries, they placed them in a context that viewed Dole as a city under potential siege, threatened by political rivals, social subversives, and supernatural powers.

At the time of Leonarde's apparition, Dole's civic and religious leaders had enjoyed almost a century free from warfare, but they feared the outcome of political and religious turmoil on their borders and inside their lands—with good reason. Dole had been besieged repeatedly in the late fifteenth and early sixteenth centuries and had been leveled in 1479 by the armies of the king of France, Louis XI. Although that event occurred 150 years before the haunting, much of Dole's population descended from the individuals who suffered at that time, especially those in Dole's mercantile and professional groups, and the city itself was still rebuilding. Not surprisingly, Dole's town council and parlementary deliberations in the sixteenth and seventeenth centuries stress the need for peace between the county's rulers and the French kings, whose territories ended a mere twenty miles from Dole.[7]

Despite the hopes for peace, the sixteenth and seventeenth centuries were often plagued by wars, and because the Franche-Comté was on the western frontier of the Holy Roman Empire between France and the Swiss Confederation, armies often marched through Dole's territory even if the city itself was not under siege. During the Dutch revolt against Spain in the late sixteenth century, the county's residents, including those of Dole, saw the Duke of Alba's soldiers march through, foraging for their supplies on their way to combat anti-Habsburg rebels in the Spanish Netherlands. Although the main battlefields of the Thirty Years' War, which began in 1618, were located in the heart of the Holy Roman Empire, the county and Dole itself were not unscathed. There was an almost constant fear that French troops would march east to conquer the province, and once the war broke out, Louis XIII of France and Cardinal Richelieu did resurrect an old claim to the county. In this time of uncertainty, the city council even worried that religious subversives, such as Calvinists, would take this opportunity to infiltrate the region further. As such, in the 1620s and early 1630s, Dole's leaders policed their borders and their community even

---

[7]From 1556, these rulers were the Spanish Habsburgs. In 1598, the Spanish and Austrian branches of the Habsburgs were reunited through the marriage of Philip II's daughter Isabella and Archduke Albert of Austria. The couple would rule both the Low Countries and the Franche-Comté during this period.

more carefully than usual. In 1636, their fears of a French invasion were finally realized.

Despite these fears, the county generally prospered under Habsburg rule and its secular and ecclesiastical elites consolidated their hold on regional authority and status. In the process, they developed institutions that placed local leaders at the forefront of any spiritual event, including the apparition of a spirit; certainly they would have fought any attempt to judge the case by any figure they perceived as an outsider, and the case's resolution would reflect on their moral claims to govern. The region's strong identity and attendant prosperity led contemporary authors and later historians to view the sixteenth and early seventeenth century as a golden age in the Franche-Comté's history.[8] During this golden age, Dole was the heart of the county's secular administration, although the imperial city of Besançon, approximately thirty-five miles away and surrounded by the Franche-Comté, was the region's ecclesiastical center. By the early seventeenth century, the region's chief legal, administrative, and educational institutions had been established in Dole for over two centuries.[9] These institutions acted as magnets for other administrative offices, and their personnel were immersed in town politics and government. Officially the county's supreme court, the parlement was the most prestigious and powerful institution, and it acted more like a council of state, supervising the ruler's rights and interests throughout the region. While its tasks were quite varied, it was particularly known as the chief criminal court and court of appeals for the region.[10] A member of the parlement (*parlementaire*) was required to have a good life and morals and have no near relatives on the court; the latter provision was frequently disregarded. By the

---

[8]Dole's parlement and university fostered a thriving historical school in the late sixteenth and seventeenth centuries; for a prominent representative, see Gollut, *Les mémoires historiques de la république séquanoise*. Arguably the most famous scholar from the Franche-Comté in the sixteenth century was Erasmus's secretary, Gilbert Cousin (d. 1572), who wrote a Latin history of the region that was published in 1552. It is available in modern French as *La Franche-Comté au milieu du XVIe siècle ou Description de la Haute-Bourgogne connue sous le nom de comté*.

[9]During the temporary French rule of the county in the late fifteenth century, the king of France had punished Dole for its defiance by removing the parlement and the university. By 1490 they were reestablished in Dole and would remain there until the county came definitively under French control in 1678. On Dole's struggles to retain the parlement, university, and other institutions, and the relationships between members of the parlement and other elites in the county, see Theurot, *Histoire de Dole*; and Headley, "Conflict between Nobles and Magistrates in the Franche-Comté, 1508–1518."

[10]The most thorough guide to the regulation of Dole's parlement is Petremand, *Recueil des ordonnances et edictz de la Franche-Comté de Bourgogne*, esp. book 1. Also see Regnault, *Les ordonnances anciennes, observées en la court souverain du Parlement de Dole*.

early seventeenth century, Dole's *parlementaires* generally belonged to legal dynasties who had long been active as regional political and social elites. From their surviving correspondence and statements in their legal decisions and deliberations, it is clear that they regarded the Franche-Comté and its communities as their personal domain, and disorder within those communities reflected poorly on their rule and threatened their claims to status. Therefore, they policed both secular and spiritual crimes increasingly in the later sixteenth century, and it would have been unusual if they did not pay attention to a spirit in their midst.

Because *parlementaires* were required to have both extensive legal experience and a basic university legal degree—although by the seventeenth century most had advanced beyond this level—the existence of a university in Dole was both convenient and complementary. *Parlementaires* came from the ranks of university professors, and professorships provided employment for the relatives of *parlementaires*. Moreover, in particularly complicated cases, the parlement would solicit legal opinions from university professors. Because Dole's university had both a faculty of canon (church) and of secular law, the town's leaders had access to consultants on almost any topic that could arise. By the early seventeenth century, the development of secondary educational institutions only enhanced the university's ability to render spiritual opinions. These new institutions worked closely with the faculty of canon law and were staffed by theologians from new and reformed Catholic religious orders who were committed to training the next generation's spiritual and secular leaders in both the latest, more humanistically inspired approaches and traditional scholastic methods. The side-by-side existence of both methodologies could lead to vivid disputes among their followers when a case arose that had both worldly and religious implications.

The connection between the organs of municipal and regional government was, however, more subtle than that between the university and parlement, and in exceptional circumstances, such as the visitation of a spirit, the responsibility for a case's management could quickly become unclear.[11] A town council, led by a mayor from one of Dole's most influen-

---

[11]The relationships between royal and regional officers and the communities in which they were based has been studied extensively for France; among the most influential works are Chevalier, *Les bonnes villes de France du XIVe au XVIe siècle*; Collins, *The State in Early Modern Europe*; and Major, *From Renaissance Monarchy to Absolute Monarchy*. In the Holy Roman Empire, where Dole was located, the relations between ruler and subject were built on a different ideological and practical

tial families, was elected annually. It governed the city and disbursed justice and patronage through the exercise of urban prerogatives and the awarding of offices and contracts. The rights to fish in municipal waterways, to collect entry dues at the city gates, and to manage the city's marketplace were all "gifts" that the council awarded along with appointments to a variety of legal, clerical, and military jobs, such as guarding the city's gates. Town offices were often held by junior members of leading clans or by clients; the more influential the position, the more senior the family member who held it. Although some families saw the town council as a stepping-stone to the more valuable, powerful, and prestigious positions in the parlement, by the early seventeenth century there were families in Dole who confined their political activities to the town council.

Given the scope of their interest and, in many cases, their years of legal education, Dole's oligarchy contained dozens of highly trained officials who brought those skills to bear on both regional and local affairs. When Dole's town council sent members to examine the woman who was seeing spirits, they thus drew on individuals with doctorates in law and professorships at the university. They approached the ghost as a legal as well as spiritual problem.

DOLE'S SOCIETY AND ITS RURAL CONNECTIONS

By 1628, the time Huguette first began seeing her vision, Dole had regained and surpassed its late medieval glory. Its population was estimated to be approximately 4,500, which made it one of the larger cities in the region, and included a wide variety of skills and trades. Shoemakers, fishermen, professors, lawyers, priests, and beggars all mingled on Dole's streets. People from outside the county studied at Dole's university; members of the powerful Fugger and Hohenzollern families came to Dole from other parts of the Holy Roman Empire to learn both the law and French, despite complaints by other French speakers about the barbarity of the French spoken in the county. The city's infrastructure had also been rebuilt and improved, with most of the main streets paved, basic drainage provided, and special areas designated for occupations deemed a threat to public health, such as dyeing cloth and butchering animals. The city's fortifications had been

---

foundation, which gave many cities greater autonomy. See Brady et al., *Handbook of European History, 1400–1600*, 2:349–84.

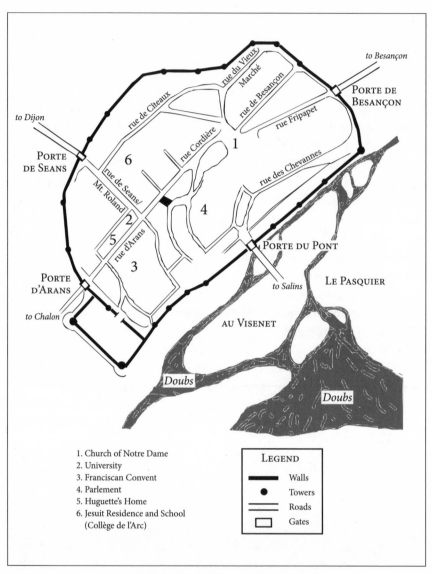

1. Church of Notre Dame
2. University
3. Franciscan Convent
4. Parlement
5. Huguette's Home
6. Jesuit Residence and School
   (Collège de l'Arc)

LEGEND
▬▬ Walls
● Towers
── Roads
▭ Gates

Dole. Map by Kathryn A. Edwards.

rebuilt, and its strong walls and reinforced gates made Dole a place of refuge for the inhabitants of the villages surrounding the city. The main church, Our Lady of Dole, was the most visible symbol of the community's rebirth. As both the physical and spiritual center of Dole—for Dole only had one parish—its destruction during the 1479 siege had been a grievous blow to the community. Among the first projects of Dole's reestablished urban government was to plan for its reconstruction. By 1628 Dole's citizens believed that the city was firmly under the protection of the Virgin Mary, and the church bearing her name dominated Dole's skyline.[12]

Dole's residents identified themselves in part through their connection to the city, and the city structure itself provided a tangible environment for their activities. Walls distinguished the city from the countryside, narrow roads forced residents into close proximity, and the few open public spaces in town were the main gathering spots. Yet Dole and its countryside were not as separate as this urban geography might lead one to believe. Since Dole was a regional commercial and administrative center, people from throughout the county, Spanish territories, and other parts of the Holy Roman Empire regularly traveled there to trade goods, get a job, find a mate, or seek medical or legal assistance. Many residents had relatives in neighboring villages or owned or leased property in those communities. Despite the distrust many rural residents had of the city, it was a necessary and valued resource in which those living around it took pride.[13]

In the city itself, villagelike social ties existed, especially within neighborhoods. The winding and narrow nature of the streets confined visibility to a small area, and judicial records provide residential testimony that this area, which they could view from their home, was thought of as their neighborhood.[14] Often inhabitants of a particular neighborhood had similar or complementary professions. Sometimes they were related to each other or were from the same village. Neighbors were also believed to have responsibilities to each other; for example, neighborhood women were expected to assist any of their neighbors who were giving birth. All these circumstances

---

[12]The most thorough description of Our Lady of Dole at this time can be found in Rance de Guiseuil, *Les Chapelles de l'église de Notre-Dame de Dole*. For contemporary accounts, see ADJ and Archives départementales du Doubs [hereafter ADD], series G.

[13]Information regarding the migration patterns into seventeenth-century Dole can be found through the marriage registers; AMDole, GG21, provides a good example. Also see Delsalle, *Vivre en Franche-Comté au siècle d'Or*.

[14]James Farr has found a similar pattern in early modern Dijon; "Popular Religious Solidarity in Sixteenth-Century Dijon."

Our Lady of Dole was the focus of Dole's spiritual life in the early seventeenth century and dominated the city's skyline. When seen from the side near the river Doubs, as in this picture, it still does. Photo by Kathryn A. Edwards, June 1999.

led neighbors to identify closely with one another, despite the inevitable tensions that could arise from living in close proximity. Even when neighbors were on bad terms, they would generally unite against an external threat. This sense of neighborliness was made official in Dole's legislation where neighbors were responsible for informing the town council or parlement of any illegal or suspicious activities in their area or by their neighbors. If they did not comply, they were considered accomplices and suffered the same penalty as those who actually committed the crime.

Similar bonds existed even in those neighborhoods where rich and poor, the prestigious and the anonymous lived side by side, a common occurrence in early modern Dole. In this case, the leader of an influential family often used the neighborhood as an established power base. In return for the support of his neighbors, he would represent their interests in town council meetings, loan them money, stand as godfather to their children, and assist them in other ways. Huguette and Antoine themselves benefited from such ties in 1630 when their son Antoine gained Antoine Maire and Carola de Marenches, members of important local dynasties, as godparents.[15] Such figures, as well as members and affiliates of influential families on whom a lesser individual was dependent, would be allowed access to most aspects of family life, effectively breaching the modern barriers between public and private space. Officials, clergymen, and urban elites could appear at a lesser individual's home and expect to be granted admission unless someone of even higher status denied it.

Another area where such personal relationships can readily be seen in Dole is in the leases to city rights, properties, and jobs, such as the management of patrols at the city's gates. They were granted at an annual auction apparently attended by individuals from varied social groups. All those interested in obtaining the use of city lands or the management of city goods, such as the fish ponds and sawmill, would meet in the square before Our Lady of Dole and bid. Because these bids were based on the projected revenues of the property, there were times when the winner could not pay his entire bid up front. Then another resident stepped in and stood surety for the bidder; if the bidder defaulted, the guarantor was responsible for paying the full amount of the bid.[16] In such ways, both vertical and horizontal neighborhood bonds were institutionalized and strengthened.

The dependency and support found in this instance is but one of many that existed in Dole and other early modern cities and reflects the personal nature of urban relationships. The city was not seen as an autonomous physical unit but as a home to people, families, and individuals. Even the structure of the city was personal, and people knew the layout of their city based on where individuals lived and where certain events happened to people. It was "the house where Huguette Roy lived" and "the house where the ghost appeared to Huguette," not the house at 5 rue d'Arans. The surviving tax records emphasize this point. They are organized to read like a walk around the city that a tax collector would take, and the way of visualizing the town they describe is based on personal networks, not anonymous landscapes. The building where they begin is often noted as the house of a particular individual; the register then moves from personal residence to personal residence. Recorded in the book is the householder's name, not a numerical street address or a physical description of the home's location. Even institutional structures tend to have these personal characteristics: the

[15]AMDole, GG15, fol. 83r. For information about the Marenches and Maire families, see de la Maduère, *Les officiers au souverain parlement de Dole et leurs familles;* and Tiburce de Mesmay, *Dictionnaires des anciens familles de la Franche-Comté.*

[16]Records of these auctions are in AMDole, 639.

seat of the parlement is known as where the *parlementaires* meet. Changes in direction are noted by marking at whose house the collector should turn or stop. The assumption is that this official or his substitute will know at least the homes of the city's leading citizens, but other records show that an even greater knowledge of residential patterns was expected of most urban officers.[17] Individuals guarding the city gates, such as Huguette's husband, Antoine, did not rely on passes and written identification to determine who could enter the city; they were supposed to recognize the city's residents and the signatures and seals of influential individuals. They were required to assess who had legitimate business in Dole, a skill that demanded a high degree of familiarity with the affairs of many people but that soldiers could be presumed to have, given the personal nature of Dole's society in the early seventeenth century.

Within the larger framework of the city, however, many other smaller communities besides that of the neighborhood existed based on a variety of criteria; guilds, confraternities, and religious houses all formed distinctive communities. Public welfare and fraternal associations (confraternities) devoted to the veneration of saints, such as the Virgin Mary, or of divine manifestations, such as miraculous Eucharists, were especially active in Dole. They contributed chapels when Our Lady of Dole was being rebuilt and endowed masses and other devotions. By the middle of the seventeenth century, when the town council began demanding that the confraternities register their constitutions, Dole contained over fifty.[18] Dole's confraternities could be male, female, or sometimes mixed, thereby promoting another form of integrated sociability. While it is impossible to tell if Huguette or her family belonged to a confraternity, their piety is much like that found in Dole's confraternities; those individuals observing them, such as Jean Boyvin's mother-in-law and wife as well as members of the town council and religious orders, would have almost certainly belonged to at least one.

Despite the integration of classes and professions on the streets and even in households, Dole's society was far from egalitarian. Hierarchy itself was seen as natural, established by God; after all, God is supreme by definition, and the angels and his other creations are subordinate. God, then,

---

[17]For tax records, see AMDole, 639. Property boundaries were often described in wills or other legal documents based on who lived or had lived on neighboring lands. Examples can be found in AMDole, 400s; and ADD, series G.

[18]Rance de Guiseuil, *Les chapelles de l'église de Notre-Dame de Dole*, 14–17.

clearly intended his creation to be ruled by a similar structure. This hierarchical conception frequently clashed with the more communitarian ideals underlying urban structures in medieval and early modern Europe, particularly in the Holy Roman Empire, and by the sixteenth and seventeenth centuries a practical compromise had been reached. A narrow group of lawyers and administrators, some of whom had mercantile roots, governed towns such as Dole. This stratum, composed of at most 5 percent of the total population, was essentially on top of the urban pyramid. Within this community, however, status and power were often being negotiated, with different individuals and households having different abilities and influence at different times, although the core group was quite stable. An urban resident achieved this status and maneuvered for increased influence through a variety of means: birth, education, profession, employment, relationships, property, presentation, and wealth were all part of the package. Below this upper rank of urban residents were many others whose relationships to each other and relative stature were also in a constant process of negotiation, giving the impression of a society engaged in an almost Boolean motion yet whose residents perceived an innate stability and order. The belief in mutual responsibilities and duties reinforced this perception. Just as God watches over his creations and his creations worship God, those in positions of authority and power had a duty to protect those who were weaker, but they also expected respect and obedience. Such was the theory repeated by Dole's town council whenever it assessed itself extra taxes or asked the city's residents for particular sacrifices. In practice, this reciprocity could collapse at all levels, a victim of class, family, and self-interest.[19]

Because of this conviction that society was based on a divinely instituted order, and perhaps because of the difficulties in attaining such order, those who apparently existed outside of that plan or who had qualities that could subvert it were often distrusted. Individuals, male or female, who changed their life suddenly or who engaged in unusual activities also fell into these categories, and their actions could trigger rapid and potentially dangerous magisterial investigations. Women who claimed to have supernatural visitors, such as Huguette, walked an especially dangerous line.

[19]For a solid introduction to these processes and the formation of urban identity on the Franco-imperial border, see the works of Thomas A. Brady Jr., especially *Protestant Politics: Jacob Sturm (1489–1553) and the German Reformation*. For the question of identity in early modern France, see especially Wolfe, *Changing Identities in Early Modern France*. For this question in the duchy and county of Burgundy, albeit for an earlier period, see Edwards, *Families and Frontiers*.

WOMEN, GENDER, AND THE FAMILY

Gender and class distinctions were closely woven in early modern Europe, and Dole was no exception to this trend. The life of a soldier's wife, such as Huguette, differed materially and socially from that of some of the women who came to observe her, such as the wife and mother-in-law of the future president of Dole's parlement, Jean Boyvin. In fact, the social status of those two women assuredly granted them the freedom to enter Huguette's home, a freedom of movement between social classes that Huguette did not share until her haunting and apparently lost soon thereafter.[20] Despite these distinctions, which were well appreciated in the sixteenth and seventeenth centuries, it could be argued that their gender, their womanness, gave them an essential similarity. Although the lives of a lawyer's mother and a workingman's wife were vastly different, and the lawyer's wife would be offended at any suggestion of commonality, during this period the activities in which both women could be legitimately engaged narrowed, and the same misogynistic beliefs tarred most women with few variations for wealth, status, and age.

In the early seventeenth century Dole's spiritual and secular leaders shared assumptions about the nature of women, and the community accepted their implication that women were inherently flawed. By this time, Christian thought essentially ignored the version of Genesis where God creates man and woman at the same time (Genesis 1:27 and 5:2) in favor of the story of Eve, the original woman, being created from Adam's rib (Genesis 2:21–25), thus stressing woman's dependent and subordinate relationship to man.[21] Based on the Adam and Eve story, Eve was blamed for original sin, for tempting Adam to eat of the tree of knowledge, although some did acknowledge that Adam could have said no. Reinforcing these beliefs was the Aristotelian theory of woman as an incomplete and improperly formed man, which had been integrated into Christian thought with the great Aristotelian revival of the twelfth and thirteenth centuries. Although these ideas were developed into elaborate physiological and theological systems in medieval and early modern Europe, all

---

[20]See BMB, Collection Chifflet, ms. 103, fols. 146r–47v.

[21]One of the strongest proponents of woman's corruptive nature was the second-century polemicist Tertullian whose writings were frequently cited in early modern Europe: "*You* [women] are the devil's gateway. *You* are the first deserter of the divine law.... *You* destroyed so easily God's image, man. On account of *your* desert, that is death, even the Son of God had to die." Tertullian, *De culture feminarum*, 1, as quoted by Wiesner, *Women and Gender*, 12.

understood their basic premise: women were psychologically and physiologically inferior to men. While women's spiritual potential was equal, these other weaknesses frequently undermined that potential and left them more open to demonic corruption and humanity's inherent flaws.

Despite the implications of this ideology, women in late medieval Europe were involved in a wide variety of activities, and those of early modern Dole were no exception. While not allowed to be a member of the major guilds, they could assist their husbands in their professions and often worked in complementary jobs, such as a butcher's wife selling offal. While the religious life was spiritually preferable and Dole's residents were enthusiastic supporters of female religious orders such as the Clairesses, marriage was another socially acceptable option. It has been argued that with the coming of the Reformation in Protestant territories, a woman's options narrowed greatly; her only valid career was that of wife and mother. In Catholic regions such as Dole, however, marriage and religious vows both remained viable options for women, but women's involvement in Protestant and radical groups led Catholic authorities in the Franche-Comté, as in other territories, to limit women's activities and supervise them more closely.[22] As in much of early modern Europe, Dole's women also found their professional opportunities constrained for economic and social reasons as population pressure led to a decline in available jobs and increased male domination of those that were available. Such male monopolies were codified in Dole's statutes during the later sixteenth and seventeenth centuries.

As the decline in women's professional activity suggests, the hierarchies that marked social life more generally also distinguished gender relationships in the early modern Franche-Comté. Gender and age relationships were based in part on emotional ties, but their hierarchy was believed to have been divinely established. It was believed that this hierarchy should be manifested in the family. In France during the seventeenth century, these ideas were institutionalized, with the French state taking on the responsibility of enforcing paternal rights to determine a daughter's marriage, to control a wife's fortune, and to leave the family inheritance to the eldest son. In the Holy Roman Empire, similar legislation was instituted but, due to a variety of factors, was less frequently and thoroughly

---

[22]There have been many excellent studies on the effect of the Reformations on women and gender roles. For current bibliographies on this subject, see those included in Wiesner, *Women and Gender.*

enforced. These perspectives were buttressed by various assumptions about the nature of men and women, some of which have been discussed above. In addition to those theories, the state saw support of familial, local, and regional hierarchies as leading to a stronger institutional and moral foundation. In reinforcing a father's rights over his household, the state's rulers imposed complementary laws over their subjects. Certainly they adopted the rhetoric. The king was the "father" of his people with the attendant rights and responsibilities. Like a child to a father, subjects did not need to understand the ruler, only to obey him, and they should assume that the ruler would act in their best interests.[23]

While in practice the husband gained increased legal and theological power over his household and relatives in early modern Europe, the relationship was not in theory purely one of dominance, even in areas now known for the traditional nature of their laws like the early modern Franche-Comté. The husband or father had responsibilities to those under his care, just as a ruler had duties to his subjects. He was bound to protect the family inheritance and invest his wife's dowry safely; if he was remiss in his duties, other relatives or, in desperation, legal authorities could step in to safeguard the wife's or children's interest. In addition, legal practice in the Franche-Comté was often far less draconian than the law itself, which demanded a woman's legal subordination throughout her life to either her father, husband, or son. She had the right of approval on the disposition of goods that she brought into the marriage and was often chosen as guardian for her children after her husband's death, thus increasing her judicial status. She could be deputized to act for her husband, and many women founded chapels or performed other good works jointly with their husbands in the family's name or independently as widows.[24] Women retained some personal property, which they could dispose of as they chose. Widows or women who remained unmarried gained the legal right to control their belongings if there were no extant male relatives related by blood; the degree of relationship remains imprecise in the statutes, but right to control a woman's goods clearly extended to the first and second generations. When allowed to dispose of personal property, women in the Franche-Comté of Huguette's class were apt to divide their goods into roughly equal parts among their heirs. Their wealth tended to be concentrated in objects

[23]Sarah Hanley's work has extensively analyzed the implications of these developments in early modern France; see "Social Sites of Political Practice in France."

[24]Gay, "Contribution aux origines du droit des gens mariés dans le Comté de Bourgogne."

essential to daily life or those that enhanced its comfort: a bed and bedding, other linens, clothing, religious objects, cooking and serving utensils, basic furniture such as a table and benches, and a few pieces of jewelry. Special attention was paid to how well something was constructed and out of what it was made. Women were more likely to receive movable property, such as jewelry or linens, and rights to income, such as annual dividends paid for loans or the use of land, but without male heirs, there was nothing to prevent a woman from inheriting everything another woman owned.

For many women with few goods and little access to legal services, however, these debates and protections remained distant to their daily concerns. More immediate were the ways a husband could enforce his prerogatives. In the seventeenth-century Franche-Comté, a husband could "chastise" his wife at will, although he was prohibited from permanently "damaging" her. This legislation was based on the idea that a woman had the same level of reason and emotional stability as a child and therefore sometimes needed the correction given to a child. In early modern Dole, a beating would be justified if a wife damaged or ruined family property, disputed with her husband too forcefully or publicly, or placed her husband and the family in a potentially dangerous situation. If a husband carried his chastisement to extremes and murdered or maimed his wife, as sometimes happened, most of the community would probably shun him and her birth family could institute legal proceedings against him. A legal fine, revenge by other family members, or her husband's punishment as a murderer was, however, probably scant comfort to a corpse.

Whatever their profession, legal status, and social qualities, women in early modern Dole were seen as sharing various interests and having certain susceptibilities based on their role as mothers. Birth in particular was a female activity, and into the eighteenth century it was regarded as obscene for a male doctor to be physically present for any gynecological examination, although he could be in an antechamber and offer advice. A doctor, however, would not have attended most women of Huguette's social class; she could expect local women and possibly a midwife to supervise the birth. In the ideal situation, when a woman was near labor, neighbors would frequently visit her, as Huguette's neighbors did. When she went into labor, the neighbor women would gather, bringing amulets, herbs, and anything else that might assist in the birth. After the birth, these women would visit the new mother for weeks or even months to help her care for the newborn and recover from any complications. Such assistance was essential. Like women everywhere at this time, Dole's women died with a sad frequency during childbirth or because of its aftermath.[25] The medical authority, the midwife, was also a member of the community surrounding the mother-to-be and could even be a neighbor. Women of higher social status shared in this procreative network; they could serve as godmothers, and the town council recruited them to police the health and sexual activities of other women in town.

In early seventeenth-century Dole, the medical profession, and to some extent the medical care individuals could receive, was in the process of being reformed and regularized. Both male university-educated doctors and female apprentice-trained midwives practiced in the city, and both asked the town council's assistance in punishing those who had not yet justified their "capacity."[26] These "professions," as they were called in legal records, worked according to somewhat different medical theories, however. Based on a form of apprenticeship, a midwife's education was practical and empirical, and her most common tools were herbs and her hands. Although they might seem to be defined by their role in childbirth, midwives and women in general provided much of the day-to-day medical care. In the Franche-Comté as elsewhere, medical doctors were trained in the theories of medicine developed by Galen and Vesalius. Key to this method was the idea that the body was composed of four humors—blood, phlegm, black bile, and yellow bile—and imbalance in these humors caused illness. Among many medical concepts that derived from this belief was that of the validity of bloodletting as a cure for fever. To an early modern medical professional, fever was clearly caused by too much moist heat in the body; removing some of a patient's blood would remove some of that moisture and heat. Although humoral properties and affinities were common knowledge and often used to enhance a treatment's curative properties, the medicine experienced by most early modern Europeans was practical rather than theoretical.[27] As seen in Huguette's story, Dole's residents were no exception to this rule.

[25] Because Dole's death registers are fragmentary and often do not contain notations about the cause of death, exact numbers cannot be known. The sense of frequency is based on a more impressionistic reading of many documents from the Franche-Comté at this time.

[26] AMDole, 177, 14 July 1628. Also see McTavish, *Childbirth and the Display of Authority*.

[27] Useful surveys of early modern medical practices and the implications of the humoral theory of medicine and the system of affinities on which it is based are provided in Brockliss and Jones, *Medical World of Early Modern France*.

Midwives and barber-surgeons had a lot of potential business because of the everyday dangers life presented. Agricultural work had its distinct hazards: animals could crush a foot, scythes could cut a leg, carts could tip and fall on people. In the city there were similar dangers and, in the case of Dole, potential construction hazards: scaffolding could collapse, wooden shingles fall off a roof, and potholes in a road be deeper than expected.[28] The cities, too, were hotbeds of disease because of the relatively high population density and poor sanitation. Throughout the sixteenth and seventeenth centuries outbreaks of plague—a generic term used for the bubonic plague, influenza, typhoid, and many other contagious diseases—frequently occurred within Dole's walls and led to the establishment of hospitals and quarantine facilities in the suburbs. The household itself was frequently the site of the greatest hazards. Most fireplaces had an open hearth with nothing separating the fire from the residents, and records abound of children falling into the fire or down a well, knocking a pot over and fatally burning themselves, or suffocating in the tight swaddling that was standard practice to assure that limbs grew straight. For women, the most deadly hazard was childbirth. Even if the birth itself went well, there was always the danger of postnatal infection, which was enhanced by the lack of knowledge about germs and by practices such as placing clumps of moss between a woman's legs to absorb her blood and afterbirth.

Given the dangers of childbirth and frequent child mortality, some historians have argued that people in early modern Europe remained emotionally detached from their children until these children reached a certain age, often somewhere around five. A complementary belief, based on the system of arranged marriages, was that couples rarely had feelings for each other or fell in love.[29] Since these theories were proposed, much ink has been spilled to disprove them, and although historians now generally agree that these ideas are extreme, they have taken hold in the popular imagination. In fact, diaries, legal testimonies, and other documents attest to the sorrow adults felt when children or spouses died. Parents made pilgrimages to assure the health of a child and hung holy medals

[28]Notations about such accidents occur throughout the town council deliberations at this time; AMDole, 78.

[29]The classic statements of this thesis are Ariès, *Centuries of Childhood*; and Stone, *Family, Sex, and Marriage in England*. For recent refutations or modifications, see the bibliography in Wiesner, *Women and Gender*, 78–81.

around children's necks to guarantee their safety. When a child or spouse died, the survivor(s) provided masses whenever possible to assist the soul in reaching heaven, and grief could even drive them to delirium.[30] Similar bonds are found between family members of all degrees of relationship and even between friends and neighbors. Bonds of family and friendship were both affective and practical, and it should be no surprise that Huguette goes into paroxysms of grief when she thinks her mother has been suffering in hell.

RELIGIOUS AUTHORITY AND CATHOLIC REFORM

The Franche-Comté's ecclesiastical structure had remained much the same since the fifteenth century, but it was not immune from the religious crises of the sixteenth and seventeenth centuries. Besançon housed the county's archbishopric, its chief ecclesiastical institution, but powerful churches and monasteries were scattered throughout the province. Dole's church of Our Lady was among the most prominent of these churches and was Dole's sole parish church at this time. It was run by a college of canons, a community of clergy whose job was to see to the spiritual and worldly needs of individuals who lived within Dole and on the lands that had been given to Our Lady of Dole over the centuries for the religious community's maintenance. The offices and lands belonging to Our Lady of Dole attracted clergy from throughout the Franche-Comté as well as from more distant lands such as the Low Countries.[31] Given this situation, it should not be surprising that some of its clergy were almost permanently absent from their post, a situation that caused resentment within Dole itself. The absentee rates for the sixteenth and seventeenth century are difficult to assess based on the surviving documentation, but complaints echoed common grievances that went back as far as the fifteenth century. In addition, Dole's residents complained about the poor religious instruction supplied by the canons and their inappropriate use of ecclesiastical rights and spiritual benefits such as indulgences.[32]

---

[30]See MacDonald, *Mystical Bedlam*.

[31]Surugue, *Les Archevêques de Besançon*.

[32]There are many excellent summaries of the early Reformation. A good starting-point for those wishing to focus more on its social and cultural impact and less on its theology is Rublack, *Reformation Europe*. See also Whitford, *Reformation and Early Modern Europe: A Guide to Research*, which has useful topical bibliographies that include surveys, specialized monographs, and some online materials.

Given community dissatisfaction with their parish church, it should not be surprising that Dole's residents commonly turned to other religious orders for spiritual guidance. Some groups had a long history within the city, while others had only come more recently. The Franciscans had been in Dole since 1372, while the Benedictines had been based at the college of St. Jerome since 1494. The countryside around Dole also hosted many monasteries, and the mother house of the Cistercians, one of the most famous and influential medieval religious orders, was less than thirty miles away. Of the three primary urban ecclesiastical communities, probably the Franciscans found the most public favor; complaints about the canons' greed and the Benedictines' laxity are found throughout Dole's records.[33] Many of Dole's elite in the fifteenth century requested dispensations to be buried in the Franciscians' church, and members of all levels of Dole society continued to make such requests into the sixteenth and seventeenth centuries. In addition, the Franciscans enjoyed municipal patronage. They gave the key Lent and Advent sermons, for which they received gifts of fish and money from the town council.

While in other provinces of the Holy Roman Empire, France, and the Low Countries, early sixteenth-century reform movements led to what is now known as Protestantism, the heart of the Franche-Comté and Dole remained relatively untouched by the troubles in neighboring territories. Known in Dole's records as "heretics" or "Lutherans" whatever their beliefs, Protestants only faced the first parlementary decree against them in 1528, and the first Protestant martyr, Crespin Petit, was executed at Dole in 1537. Despite these activities and movements to expel Protestants from Dole in 1549, 1556, and 1562, the prosecutions in Dole appear relatively mild when compared to those in other European cities. Although Dole was located on the path to Geneva, the heart of Calvinism, and such well-known Calvinist leaders as Theodore Beza passed through town, it appears that too few of Dole's council and parlement members were attracted to Protestantism for them to form an effective power block. Instead, most oligarchs allied themselves even more closely with their Habsburg rulers and were granted increased powers and privileges in the 1530s and 1540s in order to fight heresy. The existence of the county of Montbéliard, the only French-speaking Lutheran territory, to the northeast and its failed coup attempt against Besançon in 1575 only reinforced

[33]For examples, see AMDole, 78, 31 May 1596, 13 June 1598, 8 May 1599, and 13 June 1600. Later in the seventeenth century, the unwillingness of Dole's canons to reform led the archbishop of Besançon, their ecclesiastical superior, to excommunicate all of the canons; ADJ, G82.

the link the councilors made between their continuing secular authority and prestige and their support of Catholic orthodoxy. In addition, Dole's leaders could look twenty miles to their west and see the wars between Catholics and Huguenots (French Protestants) that decimated late sixteenth-century France. With these circumstances in mind, Dole's secular and ecclesiastic leaders of the early seventeenth century worried that the events of the 1500s could easily recur, despite the city's apparent commitment to Catholicism, and watched any deviation from standard religious practice with an eye colored by fear of heresy.[34]

The orthodoxy they endorsed was both traditional and Tridentine. The perceived Protestant threat led to a backlash against many earlier reform movements, and by the later sixteenth century, Catholic reform in the Franche-Comté would have a decidedly anti-Protestant tone. The cause of reform in the Franche-Comté was given firm episcopal support in 1578 when the archbishop of Besançon promulgated the decrees of the Council of Trent. The council had begun as an attempt to both reform the existing church and respond to Protestant criticisms, and many of its earlier decrees focused on weaknesses within the existing ecclesiastical structure that both Catholic and Protestant reformers highlighted. By the 1560s, the tone of its decrees had shifted and become essentially reactionary, asserting the truth of existing Catholic piety and institutions: it affirmed the role of good works in salvation, the special status of the clergy, the importance of scripture and tradition in determining doctrine, and the role of the pope as leader of Christ's church on earth. These two aspects of Trent's decrees—traditional and transformative—reflected and molded Catholic spirituality and piety in the seventeenth century. They also epitomize the religious experiences embraced by many residents of the early modern Franche-Comté.

The presence of many new and reformed Catholic religious orders in Dole and the neighboring countryside reinforced this blended Catholic orthodoxy. One aspect of Catholic reform as early as the fourteenth and fifteenth centuries had been the movement to bring religious orders, such as the Benedictines, Augustinians, and Franciscans, back into rigorous conformity to the original rules laid out by their founders. This "observant" movement continued in early modern Catholicism. Fervent leaders reformed

---

[34]Jean-Marie Dubard has written extensively about Montbéliard, the region's Lutheran outpost. Most general work on the Reformation in the Franche-Comté is dated or extremely specialized and

and renewed existing orders such as the Carmelites and Franciscans. Other reformers created new orders. Probably the most famous was that established by Ignatius Loyola: the Society of Jesus.[35] Many of these religious orders, including the Jesuits, had houses in Dole as befitted its status as the regional capital. In addition, once the French Catholic reform began, many of its leading figures came to Dole to promote their reforms. Pierre de Bérulle, founder of the Oratory of Divine Love, visited, and Francis de Sales, founder of the Visitation, preached at Dole in 1609. By the time of Huguette's visions the Capuchins, the Discalced Carmelites, the Minimes, the Ursulines, the Tercelines, and the Jesuits—to name just a few of the religious orders that had developed or reformed in the sixteenth and early seventeenth centuries—had all established themselves in Dole, and several others would arrive in the following decades. According to the census of 1635, Dole's religious houses sheltered 335 members, that is, one for every fifteen residents of Dole.[36]

This rapid growth had not been accomplished painlessly. Although there were constant complaints in the sixteenth and seventeenth centuries over the canons' simony and abuse of privileges—one even went so far as to say that they "sold the sound of their bells"—they did have many rights on which the new orders encroached.[37] The Jesuits, in particular, functioned almost as a parish within the larger parish administered by the canons. They heard confessions, gave communion, organized ceremonies, and preached eloquently to the crowds. The Jesuits' prerogative to bury in their church those who specifically requested it directly challenged the canons' rights to this customary source of revenue. Granted in direct conflict with the chapter's privileges, this prerogative triggered repeated protests by the canons. The relationships and interests of the clergy within Huguette's story need to be seen against a background of urban and ideological tension between ecclesiastical communities.

does not, therefore, take into account themes such as confessionalization; the basic work remains Febvre, *Philippe II et la Franche-Comté*. Useful collections of sources can be found in Febvre, *Notes et documents sur la réforme et l'inquisition en Franche-Comté*; and ADD, esp. 2B549.

[35]The most thorough recent survey of this era can be found in Venard, *Histoire du christianisme*, vol. 8. On the early Jesuits, see O'Malley, *First Jesuits*.

[36]Information regarding the Capuchins can be found in the Bibliothèque municipale de Dole [hereafter BMDole], ms. 131. Daniel Bienmiller surveyed the growth of religious orders in the seventeenth century and provides an exact accounting of their numbers in 1635; "Dole et la mystique du cloître." Also see Sister Marie de l'Enfant Jésus, *Carmélites d'hier et d'aujourd'hui*.

[37]AMDole, 78, 18 March 1597.

They also reflect tensions between the laity and clergy. Dole's laity at times shared the canons' reservations about the spread of religious orders associated with reformed Catholicism. Members of the university and the town council were especially cautious about admitting the Jesuits despite the support for the new order by King Philip II and the archdukes Albert and Isabella, the parlement, and the archbishop of Besançon; although the Jesuits first came to Dole in 1562 they were only allowed to establish a house there twenty-one years later (1583). Dole's leaders may have felt threatened for several reasons. When Philip II allowed the Jesuits to build a school, the university saw a potential threat to its student base. They were to some extent accurate in their assessment, although the Jesuit college would eventually become the training-ground of Dole's elites before they entered the university. Given that religious houses were normally not taxed, the town council could see them as a drain on the community it was trying to govern. The Jesuits were, in fact, only the first wave of a flood of religious establishments that eventually based themselves in Dole and raised these concerns. Dole's town council was so disturbed by their proliferation that it raised a motion at the county's Estates General in 1621 prohibiting any further foundations of religious houses in Dole, a motion that failed.[38]

Despite these fears, the new religious orders attracted all levels of Dole's society. The Jesuit residence and college were provided and furnished through the generosity of fourteen leading oligarchs including university professors, Dole's mayor, councilors in the parlement, and various prestigious legal officials.[39] Throughout the first half of the seventeenth century, the Jesuit college collected ecclesiastical benefices and fiefs from all over the territory surrounding Dole, and other religious orders experienced such pious generosity, although in smaller amounts.[40] Male members of elite

[38]Many archival sources have survived that illuminate the seventeenth-century explosion of religious orders in Dole. Some of the more informative can be found in BMDole, ms. 126 (records of the Jesuits' foundation and disputes with the city and university); AMDole, 1474 (lawsuits between the university and the Jesuits); AMD, 1583 (a royal letter supporting the Jesuit foundation in Dole); ADJ, G79 (complaints against the canons and comparison with the new orders); and AMDole, 78 (town council deliberations). Useful secondary summaries have been provided by Bienmiller, "Dole et la mystique"; Bienmiller, "Reflets de la Contre-Réforme: Dole et les dévotions populaires au lendemain du Concile de Trente"; and Bienmiller, "Reflets de la Contre-Réforme: Le chapitre de Dole et les visites pastorales." Also see Feuvrier, Le Collège de l'Arc à Dole; and Bousigue, La vie paroissiale à Dole au temps de la Contre-Réforme.

[39]Delattre, Les Etablissements des Jésuites de France, 128–29.

[40]Feuvrier, Le Collège de l'Arc à Dole, 55–58.

families endowed the female religious orders that their sisters or daughters established, as did François Bereur when his daughter, Jeanne, led the foundation of the order reformed by St. Theresa of Avila, the Discalced Carmelites, in the Franche-Comté. Their mother house for the region was in Dole, where the Bereur family was based.[41] As the Bereur case makes clear, in addition to patronizing the orders, many leading bourgeois and nobles had relatives who belonged to them, despite the repeated protests by Dole's magistrates that the religious houses were dominated by foreigners, not natives of the county. The city's residents also often turned to these orders for spiritual guidance and intercession, as did Huguette.

TRADITIONAL RELIGION AND FOLKLORE

This expansion and reformation of the Franche-Comté's ecclesiastical institutions reflect the deep Catholic piety of the Dole region in the sixteenth and seventeenth century. This piety manifested itself in ways that are often discussed as if it should be assessed according to gradations of orthodoxy, with orthodoxy being defined by the theology of the institutional church.[42] As Huguette's story suggests, however, the definition of orthodoxy and the appropriate ways it could be demonstrated were somewhat contested in early modern Dole, as they were elsewhere in early modern Europe, even among those considering themselves to be committed Catholics. One of the factors that contributed to this situation was the wide variety of popular manifestations of spirituality and the uneasy relationship between this piety and its theological underpinnings.

Like many residents of the county, those who participated in Huguette's haunting believed themselves to be enmeshed in a community that included the living and the dead, the human and the angelic. The appearance of the dead was not impossible, just improbable. This holistic view of the universe underlay traditional Christianity and justified the intercessory system and the role of good works. Saints and the less blessed dead were seen as continuing to have an interest in their spiritual and biological descendants, just as a parent or patron would support his or her children and retainers. The extent to which and manner in which a ghost participated in this community and shared in pious practices that were

[41] Albert de St. Jacques, *La vie de la venerable mère Térèse de Iesus.*
[42] Briggs, *Communities of Belief.*

widely believed to be orthodox was essential to determining its nature and its significance for Dole's residents. The support provided by the dead could take very physical manifestations, such as protecting a town from the plague and causing the crops to thrive, or be of a more spiritual nature, such as ensuring appropriate penance before death. By the seventeenth century this belief was ancient, having developed among the earliest Christian communities.[43] It led to an acceptance and even veneration of the physical remains of the departed. Not merely mementos, pieces of a saint's bones, the Virgin's milk, and even Christ's foreskin were tangible links to intangible but still present and engaged members of the Christian community.

The cult of the saints had always had a strong influence over Dole's religious life, and devotion to the saints certainly did not diminish in the later sixteenth and seventeenth century. As they had throughout the Middle Ages, saints served as municipal patrons and individual guardians; for example, Saints Hugh and Claude were expected to intercede for those named after them, Huguette and baby Claude. Like many European cities and villages, Dole was dedicated to the Virgin Mary but also paid special devotions to a series of ancillary saints. These saints were assumed to be active members of society and to intercede willingly in heaven for the orthodox. Outbreaks of plague, crop failures, and military tensions were believed to be the result of insufficient piety and led to extraordinary devotions or processions to regional shrines, such as that on the hill of Mont-Roland overlooking Dole. When the cult of the guardian angel was strengthened under the influence of Catholic reformers, it appears that Dole residents could equate their guardian angels with their patron saints, although theologically saints (being human) and angels were of different substances and had different roles in creation.

Relics were an especially visible manifestation of the city's connections to its patrons, and in the first half of the seventeenth century Dole's residents collected relics from many saints—Andrew, Aurelius, Hilary, Maxime, and Sistilie—to add to those the town already possessed. When Ignatius Loyola, Francis Xavier, and Teresa of Avila were canonized in 1622, Dole organized solemnities and processions in their honor and attempted to gain their relics, which were treasured for their sanctity and power. Even objects only remotely affiliated with a saint, such as a sculpture or an engraving of a holy image, could serve as a focus for veneration

---

[43]See Brown, *Cult of the Saints;* and Bossy, *Christianity in the West.*

and could be believed to have the same wonder-working properties as the original. The Virgin Mary had been particularly venerated in the Franche-Comté for centuries, and many relics, objects, and sites associated with her could be found throughout the county. As early as the tenth century, pilgrimages were undertaken to pray before the wooden statue of the Virgin at the Benedictine monastery of Mont-Roland, about two miles north of town. Despite the Virgin's apparent abandonment of their town during the 1479 siege, Dole's residents continued to place their only parish under her patronage and seek Marian relics. In the early seventeenth century, there was a veritable explosion of Marian veneration fostered by the Capuchins and Jesuits, and by the end of that century, devotion to the Immaculate Conception of Mary appears to have been widespread. In these ways, Dole's residents shared in common devotional patterns found in Catholic Reform throughout Europe.

One of the more powerful regional cults was that of Our Lady of Montaigu. When the Virgin Mary was believed to have appeared, seated in an oak tree, to a shepherd at Montaigu (also known as Scherpenheuvel) in the duchy of Brabant (the Low Countries), there was a stampede for pieces of the tree, which the pious had carved into statues of the Virgin and child. One of the first and most famous of these statues in the Franche-Comté was housed by 1628 at the Capuchin house in Gray, approximately twenty-five miles north of Dole. As reformed Franciscans, the Capuchins had a long tradition of veneration for the Virgin; as rivals to the Jesuits in the Franche-Comté, they likely enjoyed their control over this powerful symbol of heavenly intercession. Almost as soon as the statue was placed in the Capuchins' keeping during 1617, miracles began to occur and in 1623 the archbishop of Besançon ordered an investigation to verify the healings that the statue was claimed to have caused. This investigation was ongoing when Huguette visited the city, and it continued well into the 1630s.[44]

Dole itself possessed one of these precious statues. All of the faithful who visited Dole's image of Our Lady of Montaigu and recited specific prayers before it gained three hundred days of indulgence, that is, three hundred days removed from the time they would spend in purgatory after they died. The rewards were even greater if the same prayers were recited on the day of the nativity of the Virgin. This same statue had twenty-eight

[44]Ferry, *Vierges comtoises;* and Montépin, *Histoire abrégée des merveilles opérées.*

robes, three necklaces of fine pearls with diamonds, gold and silver chains and crosses, hair coverings of cloth of gold, and other noble ornaments, all visible manifestations of a Christian's love, respect, and veneration for the Virgin.[45] More significant for Dole's religious stature was its possession of the miraculous host of Faverney around which a regional cult developed. According to early modern accounts, in May 1608 a monk in the Benedictine abbey of Faverney set out two consecrated hosts in a tabernacle, lit votive candles, and left the church empty. That night there was a fire, and the two hosts and their tabernacle were miraculously saved. Later when masses were being said at the same church's high altar, the tabernacle holding these hosts levitated without disturbing the ashes or coals around it. This miraculous suspension lasted for thirty-three hours. Both of these events—the survival and the levitation—were seen as confirming the real presence of Christ in the blessed host, thereby refuting those who disputed the doctrine of transubstantiation, such as Protestants and other "schismatics."[46] The procession taking one of these hosts from Faverney to Dole took several days, and the cortege that met it contained all the members of Dole's religious houses, the students of the Jesuits and Ursulines, the different confraternities, the town council and all of its officers, the parlement, the *chambre des comptes* (the primary fiscal office of the county), the university, and "the entire body of the city." The veneration of Our Lady of Montaigu and the miraculous host of Faverney, and the special and Catholic relationship between Dole and the divine that their veneration signified, underscore the strength of new devotions in Catholic reform piety during the early seventeenth century.[47]

Older practices, however, continued; Catholic reformers modified some, while others remained much as they had for centuries. Many were linked to a broader doctrine called the intercessory system, aspects of which were well known to all participants in the haunting, although with different degrees of theological sophistication. One of the foundations of this system was the belief that a Christian had to be cleansed of his or her

[45]Information regarding the processions in 1622 can be found in AMDole, 3, while the grant from the papal nuncio that provided the indulgences for prayers before Our Lady of Montaigu is located at ADJura, G78. For further details about this form of Marian veneration, see Pidoux, *Une confrérie de cordonniers aux XVIe et XVIIe siècles.*

[46]Eucharistic controversies marked the Reformation from its beginning, and doctrines about the real presence of Christ in the Eucharist often distinguished denominations. See Wandel, *Eucharist in the Reformation.*

[47]Gresset, "Dole et l'hostie de Faverney"; and Boyvin, *Relation fidèle du miracle du saint sacrement.*

sins in order to ascend to heaven. Yet according to church authorities, especially Saint Augustine, this cleansing was impossible for a Christian to achieve without divine aid because of the taint of original sin. Only Christ's death had made it possible at all. What then was the typical, sinful human to do? By the thirteenth century, the doctrine of purgatory was developed in order to deal with the inherent pastoral difficulties. Purgatory served essentially as a mini-hell but with the idea that a Christian's time there could end before the Last Judgment. According to this belief, the stain of sin could be lessened through good works on earth and punishments in purgatory, although the guilt of sin remained and could only be cleansed through divine grace. The system of piety developed around this newly formulated doctrine would mold European religious life in the later Middle Ages and in Catholic provinces thereafter.[48]

Under this system, a Christian's duty and, theoretically, most powerful impulse should be to keep his or her soul in as pure a state as possible so that it could be more receptive to divine grace, and pious practices were developed to aid both clergy and laity in this quest. The seven sacraments, reaffirmed at the Council of Trent, marked the stages in and facilitated a Catholic's spiritual growth, and the sacrament of confession, or penance, was designed in particular to cleanse a Christian's soul. In order to be forgiven for sins, Catholics had to confess their sins, repent of those sins, and perform an appropriate penance as assigned by the priest who had heard the confession. These penances could take many forms and were seen as good works contributing to a Christian's salvation. Endowing masses, financing a church's infrastructure, giving to the poor, saying prayers, and going on pilgrimage were all common good works done by Christians in order to redeem themselves and were all supported by the post-Tridentine church. It was especially important that both the confession and the penances be done in the right state of mind; merely going through the form without true belief or doing them halfheartedly negated the effectiveness of the system, which was designed to make the soul more receptive to divine grace. If there were conditions set on the penances—that they be done in a certain way or on a particular day—they had to be met or the penance would be ineffective. Of particular importance in this system was the time immediately before death. Marked by full confession and repentance,

---

[48]The classic work on the doctrinal development of purgatory and its effects on Christian piety and spirituality is LeGoff, *Birth of Purgatory.* For a more recent response to his thesis, see Eire, *From Madrid to Purgatory.*

reconciliation with all enemies, final benedictions of all friends and family, and a serene manner, particularly at the moment of death, a good death was an invaluable aid in ascending to heaven and a sign of a soul's blessedness. Yet if a person died poorly or unexpectedly, all was not lost. Well before the early seventeenth century in Dole as elsewhere in Catholic Europe, a system had been institutionalized where individuals could perform penances or otherwise intercede on behalf of the dead, and those for whom such activities were undertaken tended to have personal or professional ties to their benefactor.

The importance of ritual activity and performative piety to early modern Christianity led to mixed feelings about the relationship between physicality and Christian spirituality in general. Given that this relationship was fundamental to discerning the status of any spiritual entity affecting a human—a pastoral practice and theological discourse known as the discernment of spirits—well-trained clergy in seventeenth-century Dole would have been preoccupied with the physical manifestations and affects of supernatural beings. Two general streams of thought molded the assessments of these clergy.[49] On the one hand, following a Platonic and Augustinian pattern, the body was a source of corruption, both in its physical decay and in the impulses to which it subjected the soul: desire, hunger, and all forms of sensuality. On the other hand, the body was God's creation, formed by God from clay as a necessary concomitant to his finest creation, Adam. For proponents of this principle, it was clear that God intended both body and soul to work together, although the body was subject to impulses from God's greatest foe, Satan. The debates over the importance of the body, its link with the soul and spirituality, and the value of physical remains and physicality in general underlay what were important issues for theologians and many other Christians: what would happen to the body after the resurrection; what form would the body take at the Last Judgment—its perfected and most beautiful form or the appearance it had when the person died?[50] While such concerns might

---

[49]For more specific information about the theology and practice of the discernment of spirits in late medieval and early modern Europe, see Caciola, *Discerning Spirits*; and Sluhovsky, *Believe Not Every Spirit*. Jean Gerson's treatment of this topic was widely known in areas influenced by Gallicanism, such as the Franche-Comté, and a useful contemporary synopsis of such ideas, reflecting Gerson's theology and that of reformed Catholicism, including the Discalced Carmelites, may be found in Bona, *Traité du discernement des Esprits*; and Palafox, *Lumiere aux vivans par l'experience des morts*.

[50]The standard works on physicality and Christianity have been written by Caroline Walker Bynum and Peter Brown. Although they discuss late antique and medieval movements, the questions

seem the stuff of university theological faculties, they also informed regional spirituality and spiritual guides, such as those produced by the author of Huguette's story, Albert de St. Jacques.

UNORTHODOX BELIEFS AND THEIR PROSECUTION

These more orthodox doctrines coexisted with a series of pious practices and interpretations about which the religious authorities had far more mixed feelings. Part of early Christian missionary practices had been to show that God and Christ were more powerful than the pagan gods, and it was often done through a manifestation of divine power: victory in battle, curing a leader, or overcoming infertility. In the early modern Franche-Comté, as elsewhere in Europe, the ability of God to reward the pious remained fundamental to common Christian belief and practice. The extent to which people believed they could control this power troubled most theologians, although assumptions about human ability to guide the divine will continued to govern some traditional Christian practices. For example, in the seventeenth-century Franche-Comté, while peasants were planting the fields, the local priest would bring a cross, preferably one that held a relic or communion wafer, to bless the crops. Amulets and relics were also frequently used during dangerous activities such as childbirth.[51] In this role, Christ and the saints became Christian heroes and champions ready to do battle for spiritual underdogs if they were appropriately humble and grateful and if they venerated the saint sufficiently. Saints were even seen as having specialty fields based on their own lives and martyrdoms: St. Sebastian was shot to death with arrows and became the patron saint of fletchers; St. Catherine was strapped to a spiked wheel and rolled, although this torment did not lead to her death, so she was the patron saint of wheelwrights.

Alongside the saints, who remained active in this world after their physical deaths, existed a series of other spiritual forces with which humans

---

raised and authorities cited are valid for early modern Catholicism; Bynum, *Resurrection of the Body in Western Christianity;* Bynum, *Jesus as Mother;* Brown, *Society and the Holy in Late Antiquity;* and Brown, *Body and Society.* The importance of physicality in early modern society generally is currently an active area of research; for an example of this approach, see Roper, *Oedipus and the Devil.*

[51]For further information about the magical practices used in childbirth, see Gélis, *History of Childbirth.*

had to cope, and the relationships humans had with these forces were often a fundamental part of evaluating a person's orthodoxy. The enemies of the saints and angels were the demons, Satan's minions. While the saints and angels helped humans, demons tormented them. The demons' spiritual fall from grace was reflected in their physical appearance: they were innately distorted, and even when they presented a fair face, it was only temporary or illusionary. Often some sensory sign would emerge to give the demon away. As in Huguette's story, demons were one aspect of a Christian binary between good and evil, the fallen and the saved, and ascertaining demons and their activities was one essential task of the clergy. Prominent regional lawyers and demonologists, such as the Dole lawyer and near contemporary of Huguette, Henri Boguet, made a career out of assisting them.

In the Franche-Comté, ideas about demons and their worldly role were placed alongside and sometimes integrated into beliefs about spirits who haunted forests, lost souls who appeared beside lakes, and figures such as werewolves and vampires. Living in the river Loue, about ten miles southeast of Dole, was Mother Lusine. She was half-woman, half-serpent, wore a diamond broach, and could become an aerial spirit who took the form of a snake made of flame. In the sixteenth and seventeenth centuries, there was a rumor that, in one of Dole's southern suburbs, the devil himself guarded a cave full of jewels. Many places, particularly feudal ruins, were seen as harboring white ladies; while the lady at Moissey, about ten miles north of Dole, was known for her "fantastic hunt" through the clouds above a forest, another preferred to dance in the woods until two in the morning.[52] According to both local and foreign reports, werewolves plagued the Franche-Comté, killing livestock and people, often leaving most of the corpse to waste. They had a special fondness for young girls.[53] Within the holistic Christian framework of early modern Catholicism, such beliefs were integrated into a worldview that stressed the diversity and unintelligibility of the creation. For the

[52]Thiry-Duval, L'esprit féerique; and Beauquier, Les Mois en Franche-Comté.

[53]The Comtois historian François Bavoux collected much of this regional folklore but died before he could publish most of it. His notes are in ADD, 10F. 10F56–65 are particularly useful for beliefs about spirits; 10F42, 54, and 69 cover werewolf cases specifically. Bavoux described the most famous werewolf case in the county in "Loups-Garous de Franche-Comté: Identification du refuge et observations sur le cas de Gilles Garnier." Also see Fick, trans., Mémoires de Luc Geizkofler, 123–26; and Bienmiller and Millet, Univers folklorique et sorcellerie à Dole aux XVIe et XVIIe siècles. Bienmiller and Millet borrow extensively from Bavoux and briefly discuss Huguette's haunting.

more theologically driven, these beings required classification; given that a spirit, vampire, or werewolf might exist—and few doubted that in this era—it was important to determine where it fit in the divine plan. Was it good or evil?

The techniques used to discover and, if necessary, prosecute or banish such figures further stress the integration in early modern Dole of what modern readers might separate into the categories of natural and supernatural. Spirits, demons, werewolves, and other similar phenomena were perceived as part of the natural world, albeit perversions of it. Given that the natural world was God's creation and that by definition God was the most powerful force that existed, it was considered impossible for Satan to transform God's treasured creations in their essence; the most he could do was distort or cast a glamour over them. As such, spiritual or demonic manifestations were distinguishable, intelligible, and controllable if the appropriate actions were taken. The crux of the matter was what actions were appropriate.

Individuals who experienced these beings were in a precarious position, especially if no one else perceived them. Modern scholars most commonly label as visionaries those individuals who perceive spiritual images and entities that are invisible and unintelligible to others. By its very nature, a vision is a private perception of the divine, and the visionary transgresses the boundaries used to determine appropriate actions and knowledge. They are outside "common sense." One of the first challenges facing Huguette's spiritual guides then was to ascertain whether she was a true visionary or if she was perceiving something else, something that needed to be banished from her and their town. Even if she was not believed to be a visionary, and the records make it clear that few perceived her as one in the classic sense, anyone seeing a dead person in the Reformation era faced challenges; if what they perceived disagreed with established political or religious orthodoxy, they were seen as potentially aiding and abetting the enemy, that is, the devil. Several famous Catholic religious reformers of the sixteenth century were subject to such suspicions during their careers, such as St. Teresa of Avila and St. John of the Cross.[54]

A female visionary was even more constrained. She especially needed

[54]For more detailed discussions of these themes, both generally and in relation to St. Teresa, see Wiethaus, *Maps of Flesh and Light*; Weber, *Teresa of Avila and the Rhetoric of Femininity*; and Ahlgren, *Teresa of Avila and the Politics of Sanctity*.

to receive visions that could be translated in ways that conformed to expectations appropriate to her gender, showed the virtues of humility and patience, led to penitential practices, and gave special access to God in ways appropriate for a woman. Proud or independent women who saw visions were seen as having insufficient humility; even if only the being that was experienced violated these norms, as the spirit in this story does at times, its actions and attitudes could condemn the percipient. Given that pride, humility's opposite, was one of the seven deadly sins, lack of humility could be interpreted as a sign that demons were the true source of a vision. Any such suspicion would prevent a female visionary from receiving official recognition and, therefore, official protection. Without this defense, her chances of escaping unscathed were low, especially if she continued in "unwomanly" behavior or defied secular or ecclesiastical authorities in other ways.

The connections between Christianity and the visionary experience go back to the earliest Christian events. In particular, visions were linked to Pentecost, the day fifty days after Easter when the Holy Spirit came down to the disciples (Acts 2) and established the Christian church on earth. Representations of Pentecost in sixteenth- and seventeenth-century paintings depict the disciples, sitting or standing, receiving grace directly from God in the form of a dove or flame; in the same way, the visionary claimed to have direct revelation from the source of all authority and bypassed the secular and ecclesiastical interpreters of God's word. Aware of the potential for self-deception, most visionaries, at least those whose visions have survived, were tormented by the idea that these sendings may be false, that the devil might actually be the one responsible for their revelations. Such cases were particularly complicated because generally only the percipient saw or experienced the vision, as was the case with Huguette.

One of the more famous prosecutors in the Franche-Comté, Henri Boguet, dealt with these questions and broadened their scope to include witches in his *An Examen of Witches* (1590). A chief justice in the city of St. Claude, southeast of Dole in the Jura mountains, and known for his treatise on the Burgundian law code, Boguet listed the qualities of witches and others, including those who believed they were werewolves or were possessed, who had been perverted by the devil and his servants. He then provided a step-by-step procedure for discovering and prosecuting them. While he found these individuals abhorrent for many reasons, the essence of their crimes boiled down to their distortion of nature and their natures, both

God's creations.[55] To use one of Boguet's examples, those who became werewolves endangered their soul and reason, because the wolves' smaller brains and cooler body temperatures—or so they were believed to be— would not permit the existence of a reasoning soul in that form, at least according to Boguet's understanding of contemporary medical theory. As such, werewolfism threatened the essence of humanity, God's highest and most perfect creation. For Boguet, this medical perspective proved that those who believed themselves to be werewolves were deluded and therefore were victims of or collaborators with the prince of deceivers, Satan, because "the truth is that he alone to whom creation belongs [God] can change the forms of things."[56] Although his relatives regarded Boguet's writings as extreme and attempted to suppress the *Examen* after his death in the early seventeenth century, it had been widely reprinted during his lifetime, and the continued respect he enjoyed for his legal analyses apparently led to its frequent consultation in the first half of the seventeenth century. Dole's lawyers and clergymen, such as Jean Boyvin, were well aware of Boguet's attitudes when they observed Huguette.

They also felt themselves to be battling a demonic army, of which witches were enthusiastic foot soldiers.[57] The Franche-Comté's courts actively prosecuted witches as both satanic conspirators and the instigators of evil (*maleficia*) in the sixteenth and seventeenth centuries, and the parlement was the final court of appeals for the region's witchcraft cases. The high point of witchcraft trials in the Dole region occurred from the 1590s until 1646, when Dole's parlement condemned its last witch to death. In general its conviction rates were low and its trials scattered; the one region in the county that suffered from mass panics was Vesoul, approximately fifty miles northeast of Dole. As in other areas in Europe, bad weather or disease was likely to enhance fears about witches, and in 1627/28, the region was just moving into a several-year period of famine. Many accusations derived from personal encounters; beggars denied alms, farmers trying to best

[55]Boguet, *An Examen*, trans. Summers, 23. Very little modern work has been done on Boguet, although his book received widespread praise when it was first published and appeared in at least ten editions within the first twenty-five years after its publication.

[56]Boguet, *An Examen*, trans. Summers, 145.

[57]The number of works on the European witch trials is already staggering and growing daily. The following books provide reliable yet thought-provoking accounts that set the witch trials in a broader context: Apps and Gow, *The Male Witch in Early Modern Europe*; Behringer, *Witches and Witch-Hunts*; Briggs, *Witches and Neighbors*; Clark, *Thinking with Demons*; Levack, *Witch-Hunt in Early Modern Europe*; and Roper, *Witch Craze*.

their neighbors, and childless, solitary, and elderly women were all likely victims of a witchcraft accusation. Approximately 80 percent of those accused in the county were women. Some of those accused apparently believed in their guilt and had even confessed their activities to priests and received absolution years before they were brought to the attention of the secular courts.[58] In its concerns about the supernatural, the means at its disposal to prosecute it, and the extent of these prosecutions, Dole's society was far from unusual.

In sixteenth- and seventeenth-century Europe the most common legal procedure followed the inquisitorial method—not to be confused with the institutions called the Inquisition—and the influence of inquisitorial training appears in some of the question-and-answer sessions that Huguette and Leonarde undergo. It was also one of the foundations of the legal training that distinguished Dole's elites. The inquisitorial method was based on detailed, directed, and repeated questioning of those accused of a crime by trained justices, lawyers, and at times, theologians. It was presumed that the knowledge and innate qualities that came with their class would make these judges more likely to ascertain the truth and that the unrelenting, precise questioning would be more likely to provoke revelatory lapses in a guilty person's testimony. Those accused of witchcraft or of crimes resembling witchcraft, such as consorting with demons, faced prosecution in the Franche-Comté by one of two regional courts: the Inquisition based in Besançon and Dole's parlement.[59] Independent of Besançon's archbishop, the Inquisition faced constant resentment as a rival judicial institution from both the archbishop's court and the parlement. By the end of the sixteenth century, Dole's parlement had wrested the jurisdiction over many such cases from the ecclesiastical courts and had become the court of final appeal. One argument used by Dole's officers to obtain this power was the claim that heresy was a form of high treason, a political crime as well as a spiritual one, and thus fell under its purview.[60] The county's Habsburg rulers were avid to have the men and women accused of sorcery prosecuted as fully as possible and passed four acts between 1599 and 1613 urging the courts to enforce all laws in these cases,

[58]The most thorough survey of witchcraft in the Jura remains Monter, *Witchcraft in France and Switzerland.*

[59]For more detailed information about the Inquisition in the Franche-Comté, see Tissot, "Notice sur l'établissement et les statuts de l'inquisition en Franche-Comté," available in typescript at BMDole.

[60]See ADD, 10F and 2B2373.

an action suggesting that Dole's parlement may have been perceived as lenient, at least in comparison with some others in the territories ruled over by the archdukes. Given the parlement's reluctance to prosecute, Huguette may have been fortunate that she lived in Dole.

These statutes also blurred the line between witchcraft prosecutions and hunting heretics, especially Protestants. According to these documents, people in the county could not hold opinions against those of the Catholic faith, could not possess heretical books, and could not frequent Protestant preachers. Innkeepers were responsible for making sure that their customers did not slander "religion"; they were also prohibited from serving meat on days of abstinence and were required to denounce anyone they saw doing any of these things. By not distinguishing between Protestants, dissenters, and witches in these laws, the county's officials were at least theoretically obliged to treat all equally. These laws and the ways in which they were followed also left an opening for a poor, sick young woman haunted by the dead to become an influential figure in local and regional society.

FURTHER READING

This bibliography is designed as a brief guide for readers just venturing into the field of early modern popular religion. These works give greater context for themes found in Huguette and Leonarde's story, such as family life and Catholic reform, or are themselves exemplary case studies. This list focuses on English-language materials whenever possible, but because most of the research on early modern Dole and the Franche-Comté is in French, some works in French are included.

Works on Dole and the Franche-Comté

Bienmiller, Daniel, and Michelle Millet. "Univers folklorique et sorcellerie à Dole." *Cahiers dolois* 1 (1977).

Delsalle, Paul. *Vivre en Franche-Comté au siècle d'Or, XVIe–XVIIe siècles*. Besançon: Cêtre, 2006.

Dey, Aristide. *Histoire de la sorcellerie au comte de Bourgogne*. Vesoul: L. Suchaux, 1861.

Edwards, Kathryn A. *Families and Frontiers: Re-Creating Communities and Boundaries in the Early Modern Burgundies*. Boston: Brill, 2002.

Febvre, Lucien. *Notes et documents sure la Réforme et l'Inquisition en Franche-Comté*. Paris: Honoré Champion, 1912.

———. *Philippe II et la Franche-Comté*. Paris: Honoré Champion, 1911.

Fiétier, Roland, ed. *Histoire de la Franche-Comté*. Toulouse: Edouard Privat, 1978.

Rochelandet, Brigitte. *Sorcières, Diables et Bûchers en Franche-Comté au XVIe et XVIIe siècles*. Besançon: Cêtre, 1997.

Theurot, Jacky, et al. *Histoire de Dole*. Roanne: Editions Horvath, 1982.

Walter, Hélène, et al. *Histoire de la Franche-Comté*. Besançon: Cêtre, 2006.

Works on Other Themes

Ariès, Philippe. *The Hour of Our Death*. Translated by Helen Weaver. New York: Oxford University Press, 1991.

Behringer, Wolfgang. *The Shaman of Oberstdorf: Chonrad Stoeckhlin and the Phantoms of the Night*. Translated by H. C. Erik Midelfort. Charlottesville: University of Virginia Press, 1998.

Bilinkoff, Jodi. *Related Lives: Confessors and Their Female Penitents, 1450–1750*. Ithaca, NY: Cornell University Press, 2005.

Briggs, Robin. *Early Modern France, 1560–1715*. New York: Oxford University Press, 1998.

Brockliss, Laurence, and Colin Jones. *The Medical World of Early Modern France*. Oxford: Clarendon Press, 1997.

Burguière, André, et al., eds. *A History of the Family*. Vol. 2, *The Impact of Modernity*. Translated by Sarah Hanbury-Tenison. Introduction by Jack Goody. Cambridge, MA: Harvard University Press for Belknap, 1996.

Bynum, Caroline Walker. *Wonderful Blood: Theology and Practice in Late Medieval Northern Germany and Beyond*. Philadelphia: University of Pennsylvania, 2007.

Caciola, Nancy. *Discerning Spirits: Divine and Demonic Possession in the Middle Ages*. Ithaca, NY: Cornell University Press, 2003.

Christian, William A. *Apparitions in Late Medieval and Renaissance Spain*. Princeton, NJ: Princeton University Press, 1981.

———. *Local Religion in Sixteenth-Century Spain*. Princeton, NJ: Princeton University Press, 1981.

Clark, Peter, ed. *Small Towns in Early Modern Europe*. New York: Cambridge University Press, 1995.

Clark, Stuart. *Thinking with Demons: The Idea of Witchcraft in Early Modern Europe*. New York: Oxford University Press, 1997.

———. *Vanities of the Eye: Vision in Early Modern European Culture*. New York: Oxford University Press, 2007.

Davies, Owen. *The Haunted: A Social History of Ghosts*. New York: Palgrave, 2007.

Davis, Natalie Zemon. *Fiction in the Archives: Pardon Tales and Their Tellers in Sixteenth-Century France*. Stanford, CA: Stanford University Press, 1987.

———. "Ghosts, Kin and Progeny: Some Features of Family in Early Modern France." *Daedalus* 106 (Spring 1977): 87–114.

Elliott, Dyan. *Proving Women: Female Spirituality and Inquisitorial Culture in the Later Middle Ages*. Princeton, NJ: Princeton University Press, 2004.

Fairchilds, Cissie. *Domestic Enemies: Servants and Their Masters in Old Regime France*. Baltimore: John Hopkins University Press, 1984.

Ferber, Sarah. *Demonic Possession and Exorcism in Early Modern France*. New York: Routledge, 2004.

Forster, Marc R. *Catholic Revival in the Age of the Baroque: Religious Identity in Southwest Germany, 1550–1750*. New York: Cambridge University Press, 2001.

Gélis, Jacques. *A History of Childbirth: Fertility, Pregnancy, and Birth in Early Modern Europe*. Translated by Rosemary Morris. Boston: Polity Press, 1991.

Gibson, Wendy. *Women in Seventeenth-Century France*. New York: St. Martin's, 1989.

Ginzburg, Carlo. *Ecstasies: Deciphering the Witches' Sabbath*. New York: Routledge, 1990.

———. *The Night Battles: Witchcraft and Agrarian Cults in the Sixteenth and Seventeenth Centuries*. Baltimore: Johns Hopkins University Press, 1983.

Gordon, Bruce, and Peter Marshall, eds. *The Place of the Dead: Death and Remembrance in Late Medieval and Early Modern Europe*. New York: Cambridge University Press, 2000.

Harline, Craig. *Miracles at the Jesus Oak: Histories of the Supernatural in Reformation Europe*. New York: Doubleday, 2003.

Holt, Mack P. *The French Wars of Religion, 1562–1629*. 2nd ed. New York: Cambridge University Press, 2005.

Hsia, R. Po-chia. *The World of Catholic Renewal, 1540–1770*. 2nd ed. New York: Cambridge University Press, 2005.

Imhof, Arthur E. *Lost Worlds: How Our European Ancestors Coped with Everyday Life and Why Life Is So Hard Today*. Translated by Thomas Robisheaux. Charlottesville: University Press of Virginia, 1996.

Jutte, Robert. *Poverty and Deviance in Early Modern Europe*. New York: Cambridge University Press, 1994.

Kagan, Richard L. *Lucrecia's Dreams: Politics and Prophecy in Sixteenth-Century Spain*. Berkeley: University of California Press: 1990.

Kamen, Henry. *Early Modern European Society*. New York: Routledge, 2000.

Kertzer, David I., and Marzio Barbagli. *A History of the European Family*. New Haven, CT: Yale University Press, 2001.

King, Margaret L., and Albert Rabil Jr. *Teaching Other Voices: Women and Religion in Early Modern Europe*. Chicago: University of Chicago Press, 2007.

Ladurie, Emmanuel Le Roy. *The French Peasantry, 1450–1660*. Translated by Alan Sheridan. Berkeley: University of California Press, 1987.

Le Goff, Jacques. *The Birth of Purgatory.* Translated by Arthur Goldhammer. Chicago: University of Chicago Press, 1984.

Levack, Brian. *The Witch-Hunt in Early Modern Europe.* 3rd ed. New York: Longman, 2006.

Levi, Giovanni. *Inheriting Power: The Story of an Exorcist.* Translated by Lydia G. Cochrane. Chicago: University of Chicago Press, 1988.

Lüdtke, Alf, ed. *The History of Everyday Life: Reconstructing Historical Experiences and Ways of Life.* Translated by William Templer. Princeton, NJ: Princeton University Press, 1995.

Lynch, Katherine A. *Individuals, Families, and Communities in Europe, 1200–1800: The Urban Foundations of Western Society.* New York: Cambridge University Press, 2003.

Mack, Phyllis. *Visionary Women: Ecstatic Prophecy in Seventeenth-Century England.* Berkeley: University of California Press, 1992.

Marshall, Peter. *Beliefs and the Dead in Reformation England.* New York: Oxford University Press, 2002.

———. *Mother Leakey and the Bishop: A Ghost Story.* New York: Oxford University Press, 2007.

———, and Alexandra Walsham, eds. *Angels in the Early Modern World.* New York: Cambridge University Press, 2006.

Muchembled, Robert. *A History of the Devil: From the Middle Ages to the Present.* Translated by Jean Birrell. Cambridge, UK: Polity Press, 2003.

Muir, Edward. *Ritual in Early Modern Europe.* 2nd ed. New York: Cambridge University Press, 2005.

Oldridge, Darren. *Strange Histories: The Trial of the Pig, the Walking Dead, and Other Matters of Fact from the Medieval and Renaissance Worlds.* New York: Routledge, 2005.

Ozment, Steven. *Ancestors: The Loving Family in Old Europe.* Cambridge, MA: Harvard University Press, 2001.

Ruff, Julius R. *Violence in Early Modern Europe, 1500–1800.* New York: Cambridge University Press, 2001.

Schindler, Norbert. *Rebellion, Community, and Custom in Early Modern Germany.* Translated by Pamela E. Selwyn. New York: Cambridge University Press, 2002.

Schmitt, Jean-Claude. *Ghosts in the Middle Ages: The Living and the Dead in Medieval Society.* Translated by Teresa Lavender Fagan. Chicago: University of Chicago Press, 1994.

Schutte, Anne Jacobson. *Aspiring Saints: Pretense of Holiness, Inquisition, and Gender in the Republic of Venice, 1618–1750.* Baltimore: Johns Hopkins University Press, 2001.

Scribner, Robert, and Trevor Johnson, eds. *Popular Religion in Germany and Central Europe, 1400–1800.* New York: St. Martin's Press, 1996.

Sluhovsky, Moshe. *Believe Not Every Spirit: Possession, Mysticism, and Discernment in Early Modern Catholicism.* Chicago: University of Chicago Press, 2007.

Soergel, Philip M. *Wondrous in His Saints: Counter-Reformation Propaganda in Bavaria.* Berkeley: University of California Press, 1993.

Vauchez, André. *Sainthood in the Later Middle Ages.* Translated by Jean Birrell. New York: Cambridge University Press, 1997.

Webb, Diana. *Pilgrims and Pilgrimage in the Medieval West.* London: J. B. Tauris, 1999.

Wiesner-Hanks, Merry E. *Christianity and Sexuality, 1450–1750.* New York: Routledge, 1998.

———. *Women and Gender in Early Modern Europe*. 2nd ed. New York: Cambridge University Press, 2000.

Williams, Gerhild Scholz. *Defining Dominion: The Discourses of Magic and Witchcraft in Early Modern France and Germany*. Ann Arbor: University of Michigan Press, 1995.

This building currently is at the address where Huguette lived on
the rue d'Arans [rue d'Arenes]. Some of it dates from the period of
this story. Photo by Kathryn A. Edwards, June 1999.

The History of the Appearance of a Spirit Which Happened in the City of Dole, July 24, 1628

by
Christophe Mercier
also known in religion as Albert de St. Jacques

Cast of Characters
(in order of appearance)

Christophe Mercier — wrote this account of the haunting; he appears in this text as "I," not by name; died 1680

Huguette Roy — a young woman about to have a baby who is visited by an apparition for approximately two months; died ca. 1634–41

Antoine Roget — Huguette's husband; he works as a guard at Dole's city gates; he survives Huguette and apparently remarries

Jeanne Massey — Huguette's closest friend; she lives near Huguette, helps her when she is ill, and is present throughout much of the story

Claude Roy — Huguette's son, born 9 April 1628; Huguette's suffering before his birth and her difficulties with previous children trigger the spirit's apparition

Nicolas Baussey — Franciscan friar who lives across the street from Huguette and Antoine and advises them about the spirit

Leonarde Colin — Huguette's aunt who has spent seventeen years in purgatory; died 24 August 1611

Blaise Colin — Huguette's mother; died ca. 1621

Widow Maniet — woman for whom Leonarde worked; she visits Huguette to tell her about Leonarde

Master Bobilier — owner of the house where Huguette's mother, Blaise Colin, lived

Françoise Fauche — a pious woman known to Huguette

Daniel Choublier — Huguette's host in Pesmes while she is on pilgrimage

Jean Georget — Huguette's host in Gray and victim of the ghost's most suspicious action

Jacques Deniset — Jean Georget's father-in-law

Jean Roy — Huguette's father, presumably dead by the time this story begins

First Chapter

What happened on the first day.

 A good and simple woman of this city of Dole named Huguette Roy, wife of Antoine Roget, soldier of the garrison, having fallen ill with a continuous fever and at the same time overcome with a side ache, was visited by doctors and by the midwife because she was just about to give birth. They judged her to be at death's door and urged her to prepare herself, make confession, and take communion, which she did with all possible devotion. She was alone in the house, having little help from her poor husband who earns his living in part by sleeping or keeping watch on the city walls. No one else comforted her in her illness save some good neighbor women who, filled with compassion and Christian charity, did small services for her as best they could, although they did not really fulfill the needs and necessities of the said sick woman.

The good and merciful Lord, our God, hears the sighs of the one who was earnestly crying for his aid and looks upon his good and faithful servant with all his goodness and mercy, sending her a chambermaid or nurse to make her bed, to sweep her room, and to put everything away in its place. This chambermaid not only has hands to provide private service[1] to the sick woman, but, in addition, she had a manner, bearing, and a way of speaking so sweet and so appealing and so consoling that in opening her mouth to greet Huguette, she suddenly opened Huguette's heart,

[1]The intimate personal care that a servant provided their employer. It could include bathing them, caring for them when they were sick, washing their clothes, and emptying their chamberpots.

which had been gripped by sadness and worry, making a heavenly joy and gladness flow sweetly. Moreover she acted as her doctor and midwife providing a very good and valuable service, the whole being done with divine wisdom and providence. This service, therefore, so charitable and extraordinary, began in the following way on Friday morning, which was the fourth day of her illness and the seventh of the month of April of this present year, 1628.

As the husband of the said sick woman had left the house at daybreak to be at the opening of the city gate, here enters into the room a young woman dressed in white in the style of a village woman. After having courteously greeted the said sick woman and inquired about her illness, she offers Huguette aid, asks her if it would please her, and if she would find it agreeable to have her bed made. Huguette had no sooner replied by a gesture, instead of a word, that it would cheer her greatly if someone freshened her poor and hard bed the slightest bit, than this young woman, as charitable as she was unknown, without any delay, takes the sick woman's corselet,[2] puts it before the fire to get the dampness out of it, and once it is all warm, places it on Huguette's shoulders after having gently seated her on the bed. This done she put shoes on the feet of the sick woman for want of slippers and, taking her by her two arms, eased her gracefully out of the bed and leads her near the fire. Having seated Huguette, she promptly sets about shaking out the mattress of this poor cot, properly arranging the sheets and the coverlet[3] on top. She takes the broom behind the door and, without bending over, sweeps the room with unequaled diligence, then leads the poor, feverish woman back to her bed and puts her in it with the same gentleness and sweetness with which she had lifted her from it. After which she apologizes in a friendly way for not being able to render her any other service, exhorting Huguette to have courage and to put her trust in God; then she takes her leave and departs.

Remaining all alone although comfortably in bed, the sick woman is unable to sleep much because of the three illnesses which continue to try

---

[2] A garment that covered the body from the shoulders to just below the waist. Corselets could come in many styles and fabrics; Huguette's was probably relatively simple and of wool.

[3] A form of blanket. It could be made out of wool, linen, or a more luxurious fabric and be stitched in a wide variety of patterns. For someone of Huguette's economic level, the coverlet was probably patched or quilted with pieces of different fabrics. While the stitching could be elaborate, the thread was most likely inexpensive.

her, to wit, the continuous fever, the side ache, and the illness of pregnancy,[4] and because of the service which had just been done for her by an unknown person. She began picturing in her imagination all the neighboring women and the women of her acquaintance and did not find any at all who resembled this woman.

She says to one of her neighbors who comes to visit her, "Jeanne, my good friend, do you have any idea who this woman is who came here in the early morning and made my bed and put me back in it, as you see? Oh, what a fine and charitable creature! Oh, what a diligent woman! Jesus, how gentle she is, how discreet, how capable in what she does! You know, my great friend, you know my aches and pains and particularly the great trouble that I have been having in my left arm since yesterday. She took me by the very same arm, led me to the fire, and led me back to this bed with so much gentleness that I am completely astonished about it. She's young, eighteen to twenty years old, her clothes are as white as snow, and her face red like the rose which blooms with the rising sun. I was so surprised or, should I say, so badly brought up, that at her departure I didn't give her anything for the great courteousness which she showed toward me. Oh, what a good woman! May God give her his love! Is there no way to know who she is, to thank her for this?"

"I'll inquire about it," says the neighbor, which she does right away and does not find any girl or woman in the whole neighborhood who did this service for the sick woman. No one at all who entered this small, little room that day.

"What?" responds the sick woman, "Could this be a spirit, then? Jesus!" she says while crossing herself with the sign of the cross. "Jesus, Mary, may God be my protector! Could a spirit from the other world have indeed made my bed? Could it have led me to the fire? I thought as much when that young woman was making my bed because, hearing some noise that someone was making on the steps as if someone had wanted to enter the room, she disappeared, and seeing her afterwards finish covering my bed, I thought she had hidden behind the curtain." There was no need to

---

[4]Early modern theorists saw pregnant woman as in a simultaneously dangerous and powerful state. Theories varied greatly as to the effect a pregnant woman could have on her child, ranging from the more Aristotelian perspective that a woman was a mere vessel for male seed to warnings that pregnant women should avoid certain foods, emotions, and activities because of their effect on the physical and moral state of the fetus. Childbirth itself was a dangerous process, and many people knew at least one woman who had died while giving birth.

say any more about it to let all the neighboring women know, and little by little the whole city as well, that a spirit had visited a woman in the rue d'Arans.

But the sick woman was the first of all to be convinced of this, and the opinion which she had formed about it that morning changed into certain knowledge when, finding herself alone at four in the evening, the white woman, as she was called, comes to present herself before her bed without having knocked beforehand or opened the door, which was closed, or made even the slightest noise. I leave you to think who was overcome with fright on this occasion. I firmly believe that if this poor, feverish woman had not had faith in God, supported by her good conscience, being that she was of a very fearful and timid nature, she would have fainted and died of fright, as she said immediately thereafter. But the spirit, who appeared with a gentle and friendly face, was likewise gentle and friendly in speech. When it perceived that the sick woman's burning fever had been replaced by a pale color, the spirit says, "Do not be afraid, my friend! Don't be shocked to see me! God has sent me here to wait upon you. Allow me to obey him by accepting such small tasks as I will do for you by his commandment. If it had pleased this good Lord that my power should reach farther, surely you would soon learn through good and charitable deeds the cordial affection with which I cherish you and would help you. Therefore, trust me so that I may be of the same service to you as I was this morning."

It had no sooner finished speaking than it takes hold of her dress, helps her down from the bed, leads her to a chest, settles her upon it as best it could, makes the bed, puts her back into it, and after graciously apologizing for not being able to do anything else, leaves her with God's blessing and a good evening. It then turned around with a measured and modest step to the door where it disappeared without even opening it the slightest bit.

After this second visit by the spirit, a Jesuit father was called the same day to console the sick woman so that they can take counsel from him concerning this affair.[5] Thus he comes quickly and sees the bed properly arranged by the spirit who had just left a short time before. He listens to the sick woman speak, telling him about what had happened. After

---

[5]Presumably "they" refers to Huguette and her husband, but it could also include their neighbors and additional residents of Dole itself.

Early nineteenth-century engraving showing the road alongside the Jesuit
residence and the Collège de l'Arc, where the Jesuit school was established.
Image from Alexandre Fragonard, *Voyages pittoresques et romantiques
dans l'ancienne France: Franche-Comté* (Paris, 1825).

which, having gained a good understanding of all this and supposing on first impression that this soul might be a soul from purgatory, he urges the sick woman to thank divine goodness for the service which he had given her through this spirit or unknown and extraordinary servant, and in case the enemy of the human race had dressed himself as an angel of light in order to deceive and fool her, he makes her renounce all inducements and promise never to wish to have a master other than Jesus Christ whom she worships and to whom she submits herself wholeheartedly. The sick woman is armed with the invisible weapons of faith in God, with trust in the blessed Virgin Mary and in all the saints of paradise, without omitting her guardian angel and her patron saint, Saint Hugh. She takes her rosary and puts it on her arm like a bracelet. An Agnus Dei[6] is hung around her neck with the relics of many saints; holy water is placed at the head of her bed so that she can make use of it at any time; the image of the holy Virgin is hung at its foot to stimulate the sick woman to put her trust in it, contemplating it day and night for the lamp shined there more than forty nights altogether.[7] That same evening Huguette is told furthermore to order the spirit, on behalf of God, if it returned, to say its name and on whose behalf and why it came. If it asked for masses, suffrages, and other prayers of the church, Huguette is to say they would not fail to grant them being certain that it is a spirit from God and that it is in need.

[6]An Agnus Dei could take many forms, two of the most common being a figure of a lamb bearing a cross or flag or wax stamped with this figure and made with blessed candles. The figure of the lamb was a common emblem for Christ, the lamb of God. The Agnus Dei is also a triple prayer said during mass; it gets its name from the first words of the prayer, "Lamb of God." A version of the prayer used in seventeenth-century Dole can be found in BMDole, ms. 45.

[7]This is an allusion to the length of the spirit's visitation. By choosing forty days as a chronogical marker, the author might be suggesting several possible interpretations within a Christian framework. One could be an allusion to God's power as manifested in the Flood, which lasted for forty days and forty nights, after which mankind, through Noah, was supposed to be reformed and more pure, although still tainted with original sin. A second could be Pentecost, the feast celebrating the descent of the Holy Spirit onto the disciples fifty days after Easter. Although the apparition begins before Pentecost 1628, most of the events in this story occur during that period, and like Pentecost, the visitation ends with an example of God's power and love. While Mercier here ignores this connection with Pentecost, he implies it later in the text.

Second Chapter

What happened from the second day till the tenth.

 The following day, which was Saturday, here's our spirit who returns at the same time as the preceding day with the same demeanor and with the intention of giving the same help, even to increase it. Like an experienced doctor, it assures the sick woman of her future health and puts its hand on her belly; it returns the evening of the same day and for the third time on Sunday morning. Against the hope of the doctor and midwife, at about midnight Huguette gave birth to a healthy and robust son who received at the holy baptismal font the name Claude.[8] Nevertheless the said spirit never wanted to answer the questions which the sick woman asked it according to the instructions of the reverend Jesuit father, replying in all cases that it could not do so, not having God's permission to do so.

Now these refusals aroused suspicions of something bad in this spirit, and recourse is made to the established prayers of the church to bless the house, to conjure the demons and bad goblins from places which they disturb by their likenesses. Yet even with all that, it does not desist

---

[8]It was common practice to delay naming an infant until it was baptized, and most children's names were passed through the family or were the names of their godparents. For example, in both the duchy and county of Burgundy, Étienne was a popular name for boys, and it is not uncommon to find several generations of Étiennes in a family. Also, a child was normally named after a saint under whose protection the child would be placed. The name Claude, which is given to Huguette's son, was a very common name in the Franche-Comté at this time and placed him under the protection of St. Claude, whose shrine was approximately fifty miles from Dole and was a major regional pilgrimage center.

from returning to the appointed place twice a day, that is, early in the morning and at four in the evening. People being curious, no one fails to keep themselves at the ready and be on the lookout for the hour when this good chambermaid came to do her service. Now, in my opinion, either she [the chambermaid] did not do it or else only the sick woman saw her at work, such that during the space of forty days she did not once fail to come present herself at different times each day as much to wait upon the sick woman as to rock the child in his cradle and to take his covers off him so that he got some air.[9] For, after only a few days, the mother, who had covered up little Claude swaddled in his cradle, found the cloth half turned inside out on the top[10] of the cradle and neatly arranged without anyone of this world having touched it. It is likely that God wanted in this way to warn this good and young mother to give milk to her children at night, because the two preceding babies she had had were found in the morning dead in their cradles at the age of three or three and a half months, notwithstanding that their mother had put them to bed the preceding evening in good health or at least without having any sickness of which anyone was aware.

It happened sometimes that, the child crying in the early morning, the mother takes him out of the cradle to give him her breast before the spirit arrived, and the spirit having come did not leave off rocking the cradle even though the child was not there anymore. This happened in the presence of two people besides the sick woman who saw the cradle move without seeing anyone who was moving it. And the child's mother saw the spirit move the cradle quite forcefully and, fearing that it would break it, admonished it not to do such things being that they were useless and could be hurtful. It replied that it would not break the cradle and it was not useless to obey God who had sent it there for this purpose; it would not have moved the said cradle with so much force if the child had been lying in it as he should have been.

As for sweeping the room, the sick woman alone saw this spirit take the broom from behind the door, near the hearth, or even between the sideboard and the head of the bed where she hid it on purpose to see if the

[9]In early modern Europe, babies were frequently swaddled (wrapped tightly in cloth or a blanket). Not only was it believed to help babies' limbs grow straight, but it prevented infants from injuring themselves while mothers and other caregivers were doing the many tasks necessary to an early modern household.

[10]Based on this passage, Claude's cradle was probably similar to a modern bassinet where the front third of the cradle curves upward, forming a cover to protect an infant's head from rain or the sun.

spirit would find it. She saw it sweep with skill without stooping, and those who could not see the broom when the spirit moved it heard the noise of the said broom from sundry places and saw the room clean and the garbage sometimes behind the door, other times at the hearth, and now and then in the middle of the room when the said spirit was surprised because of someone arriving unexpectedly in the same room.

It also happened that the neighbor women of our sick woman, when they said good evening and good night to her, left everything in the room in disarray in order to test if the spirit would put something away. In the morning they found everything as they wished. For example, the pitcher which they had left on the table, they found it on the sideboard put away with the other dishware. The tablecloth which they had left completely unfolded with crumbs on the table, they found it folded, and the said table was as clean and shining as if it had been waxed. Among other things one evening an ewer and a wine pitcher had been placed almost at the two extreme ends of the room. The following morning, the ewer was found right next to the pitcher touching the bed which the spirit had made. No one saw the spirit do this save the sick woman who was often astonished at the readiness of this young chambermaid or white woman[11] to shake the mattress, hang out the bedsheets, [and] arrange the coverlet and her dexterity in lifting her, leading her back, and putting her back in bed as we said above.

I do not want to refute here those who would say that it is Huguette who made the bed and made you believe that it is a spirit, for he who considers carefully the very high and continuous fever that burned her, the sharp pain or side ache which took away almost all of her breath and her breathing, and her pregnancy which made her almost immobile and without arms for such exercise during the first three days of this help, he will easily believe that a poor body, stricken with the three ills that we have just named, would not have been able to make this bed nor, by the same token, would any other person of this world whatsoever. All the more so since on several occasions and particularly on the day of the Invention of the Holy Cross,[12] we all saw the said Huguette having been taken out of bed and led

[11]Throughout this text when the spirit is referred to as a "white woman," it should not be viewed as a comment on her ethnicity, but as a mark of her purity. There was a long Christian tradition of holy women, especially the Virgin Mary, returning to this world either dressed in white or radiating such light that everything about them appeared white.

[12]A solemn religious holiday on 3 May, it celebrates the finding of the True Cross two centuries after Christ's resurrection.

to the room of her good friend and neighbor, lady Jeanne Masle,[13] and we all saw, I say, a quarter of an hour later the bed made which had been left in complete disorder. During this time the door to the room was closed and no neighbor, female or male, nor anyone else whatsoever entered it. Things being thus, I beseech you, who can have done this task so quickly behind a closed door if it is not the spirit or the white woman who said she was sent by God to wait upon her who put all her trust in him?

[13]This is the same neighbor mentioned as "Jeanne" in chapter 1. In the manuscript, her last name is spelled in three ways: Massé, Massey, and Masle. In this era many authors spelled phonetically, which could account for the variant spellings of her name. The difference between the last spelling and the previous two probably came about through a transcription error. It was common in this period for s to be written with a long stroke with a slight curve at the top and bottom. When copying this document, Leonel Dusilet likely confused the s with the l in Mercier's handwriting.

Early nineteenth-century engraving of the gate to the Franciscan convent located across the street from Huguette's residence. Because of the narrowness of the rue d'Arans, the building appears less monumental in reality. Image from Alexandre Fragonard, *Voyages pittoresques et romantiques dans l'ancienne France: Franche-Comté* (Paris, 1825).

Third Chapter

What happened from the tenth day till the twentieth.

 If I did not fear being too long-winded, I would tell you all about what happened one morning in the presence of Brother Nicolas Baussey, a Franciscan. Thus I will not tell you how master Antoine Roget, Huguette's husband, seeing that the Jesuit father did not come there though he had been called, asked this good friar to come to his house, which faces their convent, in order to be a spectator at that which might take place between the spirit and his wife or, rather, to chase it away from there with psalms from his breviary,[14] with Hail Marys[15] from his rosary, or else with his blessed cord,[16] which he rightly believed ought not to be touched by a damned spirit if this indeed was one.

Thus charity makes him forego the little rest that he would have taken at the convent. Having come to keep watch with his neighbor, he spends almost the whole night in prayer in order to prepare himself for

---

[14]A book of canonical prayers recited daily by priests or members of religious orders.

[15]The Ave Maria, known in English as the Hail Mary, was one of the most popular Catholic prayers in the seventeenth century, although it had only been given official form at the Council of Trent. It formed part of the most common prayer cycles, including the Angelus and the rosary. Unless otherwise noted, all translations of prayers and hymns come from *The Roman Breviary: An Approved English Translation... of the* Breviarium Romanum (New York: Benziger Brothers, 1964).

[16]The cord Franciscans used as a belt around their robes; this characteristic article of clothing led the Franciscans to be known as *cordeliers*, or those wearing a cord, in French.

the sight of a spirit clothed in an aerial body or in some other material of which a spirit can be made. He prays, he chants psalms, he devoutly recites his rosary, which had touched more holy bodies than the number of its beads. And then he put it into Huguette's hands, telling her, "When the spirit comes, boldly give it this rosary, and if it has the courage to take it, believe that it cannot be an evil spirit, and don't fail to call me as soon as it comes."

The said friar, overcome with sleepiness at around two or three in the morning, resolved to get some sleep leaning on a chest and, in order to rest more comfortably, he untied his cord and hung it on a bedpost saying to himself, "This spirit will never take my cord." This done he makes himself as comfortable as he could on this chest and goes to sleep.

Our spirit was not far from him when he was speaking about it. Here is its hour approaching! It enters, finds the household sleeping, to wit, the Franciscan friar, master Antoine Roget, the sick woman alone in her bed, and little Claude in his cradle. In order not to waste time waiting for Huguette to wake up, it put the ewer with the wine pitcher, which had been intentionally separated. It takes the Franciscan friar's cord and bends it into the shape of a cross with bends so subtle that, upon being straightened out, he could never again put it into its prior form. It hides the cord, thus bent, in the cradle under the child's bolster and puts a saltcellar full of salt at the foot of the same cradle and inside of it.[17] Some people wanted to conjecture from this that this small child would someday be a good and devout Franciscan. That done, the sick woman wakes up and the spirit shows itself to her in its ordinary aspect, coming quietly from the door without any noise. Noticing it, she suddenly crosses herself with the cross of the rosary of this good friar who was there present but asleep. And so she calls out to him, "Father, Father, the spirit's here."

"Where is it?" says the friar. "Let me see it."

"Eh? Don't you see it?" says Huguette. "It is so beautiful, so white, so modest, so fittingly attired. It is holding its arms in the form of a cross one

---

[17]Salt has a long history in popular religious practices related to its preservative properties. Salt was sprinkled to propitiate the gods and to assure luck and prosperity. In Ezekiel 16, an unsalted infant was said to be cursed, causing it to be abandoned in the fields; by implication, sprinkling salt on an infant assured its continued value and prosperity. By the late fifteenth century, salt had been explicitly linked to protection against witchcraft and other magical practices in demonological treatises, and this connection would continue through the seventeenth century. Salt was also used as part of the baptismal rite. There the person about to be baptized, the catechumen, was given salt that had been sanctified before he or she entered the church for baptism. In this case, the spirit's use of salt may allude to several of these meanings.

upon the other, its eyes half open and as if smiling to itself, its gown is completely white and flows to the ground."

"But where is it?" replies the friar, rubbing his eyes. "Where is it? Oh, let me see it!"

"Here it is beside me," she says, "right next to this small table that is beside the bed."

No matter how wide he opened his eyes, he never saw it, nor could see it. He blurted out, "For my part, I must be completely blind since I'm unable to perceive this colored and illuminated form which has the shape of a body!" He says to Huguette, "Give this rosary you have in your hands to this spirit so that I may know whether I still have some little bit of sight left or not."

The woman obeyed, and the spirit did not fail to seize the said rosary right away. The friar, who could not see a thing, clearly saw his rosary stretched taut in the air held at the end with the cross by the sick woman and at the other, where there was a skull, by the spirit, without him seeing, nevertheless, either the arms or the hands holding up the said rosary. And what surprised him the most is that the spirit pulled so hard from its side that it seemed to mean to tear the rosary from the sick woman's hands.

Seeing this, the friar said to Huguette, "Let go of it! Let the spirit have it, I tell you! It doesn't matter! Let it carry it away. I give it to it with all the blessings in the world. I make it a present of it on condition that it prays for me and obtains for me by its prayers the grace of devotion before the Holy Virgin, my good lady and mistress."[18]

"I wouldn't dare," says Huguette, stiffening her arm trying to hold onto it. "I wouldn't dare. You would be too angry with me if it were to take it away, it being so precious to you because of the holy relics which it has touched and the blessings of Rome."

While still talking she tears it from the hands of the spirit, invisible to everyone else but her. The same friar indeed saw at the same time the cradle move all by itself. The mother, who was holding the child in her arms, saw the spirit who rocked it, complaining that it rocked it too forcefully as has been said above. It [the spirit] did not make the bed or sweep the room in any way this particular morning because of the people who

---

[18]The friar wants the spirit to intercede on his behalf in the presence of the Virgin Mary in such a way that the Virgin accepts both his service and devotion towards her. In both the phrasing and the sentiment given here, the friar blends two concepts of grace: divine grace and grace as found in judicial theory.

were in the room but, stretching out its hand and its arm over the bed, gave the blessing to the sick woman according to its custom and withdrew.

The friar also decided to depart in order to be back at the hours of prime[19] and to sing them devoutly with his brother friars, but he could not leave there as soon as he wished because, as he went to take up his cord from the place where he had put it, he did not find it [there] nor nearby, which gave him pain because he believed that the spirit might have carried it away outside the residence. And on the basis of this, everything was turned topsy-turvy, inside out, and upside down in looking for this blessed cord, which was found there where it was least expected, to wit, under the little child's bolster when someone wanted to change him. The friar thus left well assured that a spirit from the other world had been in this room, with the opinion that it was good and from God, and no longer attributing everything that had happened up until then to imagination or fantasy.

---

[19]The second of eight canonical hours for prayer that were part of a liturgical day. Prime was the first hour that occurred in full daylight, generally around 6 AM.

Fourth Chapter

What happened the twenty-first day.

The rumor went around that this spirit was warlike and noisy, and this because of a sword which it was said to have fixed to the ceiling. To this I reply that, in the first place, during the fifty-three days it came into Huguette's room, there is not a living soul on earth who can say in truth that it ever made the slightest noise in the world, neither entering nor leaving, save when it was sweeping or shaking out the bed. And with regard to the sword, it is true that one morning it took it from the place where master Antoine, husband of the sick woman, had put it according to his habit and hung it by its hilt on an iron hook that was on the ceiling, which troubled in some way the said master Antoine, who had a certain apprehension and horror of taking up his sword again. Nevertheless, he was obliged to, having only that one and needing to get himself ready in order to be at the opening of the city gate.[20] Huguette, so upset at having seen her husband vexed and indignant at the ghost to the point of leaving the house and changing residences, did not fail to tell all of this to the spirit at its first visit and asked it why it had taken her husband's sword from its accustomed place. It responded that it was to warn him about his duty, because he had promised to be more diligent when he arose in the morning and to go retrieve the keys[21] in order to give it the leisure to make her bed and to arrange all

---

[20]There were actually four gates in Dole at this time: d'Arans, de Besançon, du Pont, and de Seans. The closest to Huguette's home was the porte d'Arans [d'Arenes].

[21]To the city gate.

other things as it had been ordered [and] which it could not do with him present. He had forgotten about this duty and had done nothing about it. That is why it beseeched him urgently to be more diligent, and it would not become angry anymore, as indeed it didn't, provided each one fulfilled his duty. You will be informed here that the spirit was so careful while working not to let itself be seen by anyone other than the sick woman that toward the end of the forty days, it closed the door of the room from the inside so as not to be seen nor interrupted in what it was doing.

Fifth Chapter

What happened the twenty-second [day] till the thirtieth.

 We said above that, in order to keep the sick woman more reassured, relics of the saints were hung around her neck and images were fastened around her bed, among others that of St. Ignatius, founder of the Society of Jesus, the number one enemy of demons, whose name alone terrifies them and puts them to flight. The spirit was never afraid of this holy name, less of his portrait or image, which it unfastened from the bed to put on the child. The sick woman gave it relics to kiss, touch, and worship,[22] one of the holy things consecrated and dedicated to God. It does not refuse; rather it vouches to cherish and accept them as much as she does, takes them, kisses them, and invokes them. It kneels in the middle of the room in front of an image of Our Lady of Montaigu and recites some prayers accepted by Huguette, among others "Et beata viscera mariae virginis quae portaverunt aeterni patris filium; ave maris stella etc.; O Gloriosa domina" and the Hail Mary up to and including the word "nunc" without going any further.[23] Asked by the sick woman why it did not say the rest, it said,

---

[22]Mercier's choice of words illustrates the slippages that could occur in communicating early modern Catholic doctrine. Only relics of Christ himself could be worshipped and even then as representations and, to some extent, embodiments of Christ. All other relics only received the veneration appropriate to that which they represented.

[23]These Latin phrases are from a series of well-known prayers and songs focusing on the Virgin Mary.

"The time is past, because I already felt the favor and intercession of this blessed Virgin at the hour of death."

It takes the said image in its arms and kisses it with a completely loving and filial tenderness of heart and takes the crucifix, also kissing its feet and hands. At that moment while prostrated on both knees, it said these words, "My God, my savior, true God and true man, I worship you and thank you for dying on the cross for me. Jesus, son of David, by your sacred death and passion have pity on me." It thus does all that a Christian soul clothed in a mortal body could do, adding to those above the Miserere Mei Deus[24] which it recites in its entirety, doing an act of contrition,[25] giving all the signs and marks of a good spirit in everything it has said or done in its movement, in its gait, in its white clothing, in all and by all.[26]

In order to be more assured, Huguette is told to pay attention to its hands and its feet and its head, if maybe she did not see any nails that were too long, like the talons of some bird of prey or of harpies from hell, if it did not have any bristling hair on its head in the shape of the horns of a kid or goat, because a demon would not be able to appear for long in the guise of a man without mixing into it the appearance of some wild clawed, beaked, tailed, or horned beast or to make itself known by some hissing of serpents, lowing of bulls, barking of dogs, roaring of lions, and other similar cries and howls. At other times, it stirs up in the air some stinking smell that one knows well could only come from the infernal tongue. Sometimes also, by unseemly and dishonest objects, it disquiets the feelings and imagination and excites the sensitive appetite by phantoms and lewd representations until it disturbs one's reason and makes one consent to sin, which it cherishes as much as good people hate and detest it. Now, no one ever perceived from this spirit anything which was the slightest bit distant from the truth and from direct reason and Christian modesty, never the least alteration in the body of whoever it is, never any turmoil in the soul. It seemed rather that this room was some kind of place of devotion from whence people left enlightened and consoled in Our Lord, indeed encouraged to do good and to serve God better than they had ever done.

---

[24]The famous prayer based on Psalm 55.

[25]It is unclear from this sentence whether the spirit recited the prayer known as the Act of Contrition or actually performed an action marking its repentance, although the latter is more likely.

[26]This phrasing resonates with the liturgy of that era and was probably chosen by Mercier with this effect in mind.

Sixth Chapter

After the thirtieth day the spirit declares that it is Leonarde Colin. Huguette thinks it to be her mother.

 Our spirit begins its visits by speaking, greeting the sick woman, inquiring about her health, offering her its service, encouraging her to trust in God, giving her the hope of healing, saying prayers and other words which we have already said, even apologizing for something for which it was in no way guilty, as when Huguette told it one day that it was a lying spirit because it had said to her that it had never failed to visit her twice a day from the first time that it appeared to her, yet she had not always seen it.

"You did not see me sometimes," it said, "even though I came, for I came invisibly because of the people who were continually in this room, not having the power to do anything in their presence, unless God allowed me to."

This spirit, I say, who was only from God and who spoke rather freely in some thing[s], could not say a word when it was asked if it was in pain and if it wanted some masses, prayers, or suffrages for the lessening of its pain. This one could not say its name—God not allowing it to—finally after thirty or so days it declares that its name is Leonarde Colin.

"Leonarde Colin," says the sick woman. "Certainly I don't know who you are, my good woman. Tell me something else so that I may be able to know you; otherwise I'll believe that you are a lying spirit." It replies that it

70

can say no more, and giving its customary blessing over the bed, it departs.

The two words, Leonarde Colin, remain however etched in the memory and mouth of the sick woman who ruminated to herself and comes to recall that her mother was descended from the Colin line. Completely overcome she cries out, "Good God, sweet Virgin Mary! This woman, is she not my mother who died around seven years ago, who maybe is being held in the pains of purgatory and wishes to have her pains eased? Yet she's asked nothing of me. Alas, who could assure me that this was my mother and that she needs the suffrages of the church or of someone or of some of my services to deliver her from the suffering which she endures? If I had to go to St. James, yes, to St. James,[27] to Rome, to Jerusalem, indeed, everywhere, right now I would set out, however sick, in order to pluck my mother from the pains! I would rather sell all that I have in this world, even the corselet on my back, which I say I would give away with all my heart most certainly for her who gave it to me! Oh, my good mother, are you plunged into the fire of purgatory? Is it really possible that for these last seven years you have been boiling in these flames? If only you had told me thirty days ago that you were my mother and that you boil in this fire, I would have had privileged masses[28] said earlier by all the convents and religious houses of this city! I would have applied indulgences; I would have said so many rosaries in honor of this blessed Virgin that she would have had compassion for you! Jesus, Mary, my poor mother! Seven years! Seven years and more in the fire of purgatory, so burning, so penetrating! Ah, if you had told me, I would have melted into tears from crying and would have begged my God to pour them on this flame in order to put them out or at least to give you some small refreshment!"

After these just sentiments, she is drowsy, more from sadness and weakness than by the vapors which could only come forth from a completely empty stomach and rise to the brain to put her to sleep.[29] She sleeps a little, then wakes up talking to herself, "Jesus, what a fool I am! Where is my memory? Where are my wits? Where is my judgment? My

---

[27]St. James of Compostela, a famous medieval pilgrimage site in Galicia (Spain), approximately 976 miles from Dole.

[28]Masses that earn special spiritual benefits for those who have them said and/or those who are designated beneficiaries. In this case, these masses were seen as particularly meritorious works and, if they were said on the spirit's behalf, would allow it to leave purgatory and ascend to heaven sooner.

[29]Early modern medical ideas were based on the humoral theory of medicine. Human beings were composed of blood, water, yellow bile, and black bile, and good health involved maintaining the correct balance between these humors.

mother was definitely one of the Colins of Taxe.[30] Her last name was Colin, but she was Blaise Colin. That was her real name, Blaise Colin, by my Lord, not Leonarde Colin. God be praised, it isn't my mother! If it is some other of my relatives, I know nothing about it. I have no knowledge of it."

However, here's a neighbor lady who comes into the room and learns from Huguette what the spirit told her and that its name was Leonarde Colin. Soon everyone knows it throughout the whole city and in the countryside up to two leagues[31] around. Everyone tells everyone else what he knows about it. Among others, a virtuous woman, the widow Maniet, having heard this Leonarde Colin spoken of, took the opportunity to come and visit the sick woman and told her that this spirit could well be her aunt, sister of her mother, who died around seventeen years ago, the twenty-fourth day of the month of August in the year 1611.

"Huguette, my daughter," said this good woman, "your aunt, Leonarde Colin, was a very devout woman who willingly spoke about God, always carried her rosary in her hand, and was exceedingly useful. This is why I became fond of her and often wanted to have her in my house, as much to talk with her about things of the other life and about sermons that we had heard as to serve me in the city and the fields for all that I needed there, since she was always diligent and faithful in everything she was asked to put her hand to. She took sick in my service, the sickness of death, for I had sent her to Entrepigny[32] in order to see to the harvest, and on the eve of the Assumption of the Glorious Virgin,[33] after having fasted with the most pure devotion in honor of the same lady, without eating another thing save some fruit and drinking some water, she fell sick of a dysentery that laid her very low. In order not to be cared for in the village, as was appropriate, and believing that she would be better cared for and consoled in the city, she had herself drawn on a cart here to her sister, your mother, who was living at that time in the house of master Bobilier. But it was too late because the cart shook and jostled her so much that the humors poured out from her entire body and reduced her to the point of death. Not so much, however, that she forgot herself and her salvation, because she

[30]Approximately twenty miles from Dole.
[31]Approximately ten miles from Dole.
[32]Approximately eight miles from Dole.
[33]The Assumption of the Virgin was the principal feast honoring the Virgin Mary, held annually on 15 August. It celebrated Mary's death and her assumption into heaven, although her bodily assumption did not become Catholic dogma until 1950.

quickly asked for confession and made confession as best she could, my lord the vicar having hurried there. And once she received absolution, they were about to apply leeches to her in order to dissipate and divert the humors, at which time she died. And the little which she had amassed, which consisted of the sum of sixty and some odd francs and some furnishings,[34] was placed in the hands of your mother as her legitimate heiress. And I know well that she loved you tenderly."

"May God give her peace!" responded Huguette. "May God be pleased to receive my good aunt in his paradise! In truth, I was so young when she died that I hardly remember her. You have obliged me to you, lady, by having enlightened me on this point. Maybe God will have made you speak the truth. I beseech divine goodness that it pleases him to give you some good issue in this affair."

---

[34]An inheritance of this amount would mark Huguette's family as poor but certainly not destitute.

Seventh Chapter

From the thirty-fifth day to the fortieth. The spirit says that it cannot write and makes a sign of the cross as a mark of its goodness and consoles Huguette concerning some calamities.

 The next day Huguette, more bold than ever, very content to be visited and served by people from the other world, people of her acquaintance and her nearest relatives, proceeded further in the questioning and asked if it was true that she was her aunt Leonarde. And the spirit said yes.

Huguette: "And why did you appear to me who am fearful and frightened rather than to others who are courageous and who are more closely related to you than me, like Catherine Fremiot, whom you know well?"

Leonarde: "God wished it thus. It was also because I gave both your mother and you the little that I had amassed through my modest labor."

Huguette: "What do you expect from me then?"

Leonarde responds, "I can't tell you at this time. God has not yet given me the power."

Huguette: "I pray to that divine goodness that it pleases him to give it to you so that you may be comforted soon and I freed from your visits. Not that they're disagreeable to me and not if it so happens that you are my good aunt, but because everyone comes here to weary me, filling my head with thousands and thousands of kinds of false gossip which runs through the city and everywhere about you and me. Some are saying that I am a hypochondriac or else a lunatic, others that I purposely make up what I tell them concerning your speech, actions, and demeanor. They come here exclaiming to me that you are a black spirit, even though you're dressed all in white, that you have horns under your hair and claws at the end of your feet and hands. And it's said in good French that you are an angel of darkness who appears thus as an angel of light in order to fool and deceive me. It's said that, at the end of it all, you'll wring my neck and that of my child, and the ending of your visit will be nothing other than that."

Leonarde: "Have a little patience, Huguette, my daughter, and don't be surprised by what people say. Thanks be to God, although you are a poor and simple woman, nevertheless you are a woman of good and healthy judgment, judged so by all those who know you—some for months, some for years, some for your entire life—and by my lords the doctors who vouchsafe, according to their science and in good faith, that you are one of the wisest of women and of the most steady and temperate for your station that they have seen, I say, even at the high point of your sickness during which you never uttered an inappropriate word. Do not fear people, then, when they reprove you for those things. Furthermore, if you are accused of false pretenses in order to deceive, your simplicity and innate goodness, your prayers, and your fear of God will allay everyone's suspicions and will make them believe, a human and reasonable belief, that this apparition is not made up out of your fantasy alone in your head without any foundation on your side. Going even farther, they believed and judged it to be as they themselves imagined it, making their dreams public, if I may say so, with much indiscretion, with little fear of offending God, their own conscience, and that of those close to them. Huguette, my dear niece, those who accuse you of deceit in this affair, judging your intention sinisterly, have gravely offended God, who becomes irritated when men, blind even to external things, enter into the most secret cabinets of the heart of someone near them and, seating themselves on the throne of the Creator, pass judgment on his intentions, known to his majesty alone. The conscience, also, of these people for having rashly usurped God's authority and having erred in a thing of importance and remaining tortured, tormented, and left for dead....[35] Those who have offended God

---

[35]Leonarde seems to have lost track of the thread of her argument and does not complete the sentence. It may also reflect an error in composition or transcription by Mercier or Dusilet, respectively.

in their conscience, in what I've just said, have also offended you. But it's of little consequence, you'll tell me. I grant you that, but in addition they have offended master Antoine Roget, your husband. Your relatives, your friends, and good women neighbors are concerned here as consenting to this deception that they imposed on you. Your spiritual father is also slandered in this, either from connivance or from ignorance, as if he hadn't had sufficient knowledge of your interior state to train and govern you in conformity to the will of God. My lords the magistrates have even their share in this slander as accused of negligence and lack of care in providing for the public weal and in remedying faults so important as these ones, if it [this deception] was as true as it is made up in the fantasy of your accusers. Thank God there are no faults at all on the side of anyone save their own! To make you see the care and vigilance of my lords the magistrates to prevent any evil from happening, remember that so and so[36] came the day before yesterday, appointed by the magistrates to learn about the facts; men capable in their duties would have noticed any fraud or deceit. I'm assured that, making their reports, they would have quickly taken care of this evil. So, therefore, my dear friend, you are guiltless in all of this, make no mistake, because of words which you need to let blow with the wind. Do you want to do good? Pray for them as I do and will do more ardently when I am in paradise. Good-bye for this hour."

Huguette: "All that you told me yesterday is very good, but if you are such as you say and not as others imagine you to be, give me irrevocable proofs of your goodness. Ah, here is some paper on the table. Here are some quills and some ink. Write down the purposes for which God has sent you here."

Leonarde, who had previously excused herself from writing, prays once again that no one press her more about this because she does not have the power to do it. She is asked if she has her good angel beside her. She responds yes and that it directs and leads her everywhere she goes.

"I do not see it," says Huguette.

Leonarde: "It isn't as necessary for you to see it."

Huguette: "If it's true that your good angel is beside you, beseech it to write for you seeing that it knows how to and can do it."

[Leonarde:] "But God doesn't wish it."

Huguette: "My request is reasonable so that people believe, seeing

---

[36]The town council did appoint two members to report on the happenings at Huguette's home, but their names are not specified here or in the council's deliberations; AMDole, 78, 1628.

that no one sees you and hears you speak other than me. If you ask some-thing of me, those who have responsibility for my conscience will not allow it to be granted if they have no other proofs of your word. They will never believe me."

Leonarde: "I mean to lead you to some beautiful place. I wish us to make two or three pilgrimages together."

Huguette: "You have spoken well about the pilgrimages. So how could I travel with a fever, burdened with a small child?"

Leonarde: "Have courage! God will help you! Health will return!"

Huguette: "Although the fever may leave me later and you make me see the glory of paradise, I will not take a single step to enter therein if my confessor doesn't order me to. Seeing that you cannot write, make a cross either on the cross of his crucifix, which he left me, or else on the paper that is here. Your quill will be of white, red, or black chalk. Here are all three kinds. Choose the one that pleases you, and when they see the mark made by your hand, maybe they will believe you and me also."

Leonarde, who had demonstrated during the preceding days by many exterior acts that she loved the cross, kissing the feet and hands of the crucifix, worshipping it and crying mercy, striking her chest, pros-trated in front of it, could not in good faith refuse to render and mark down this salutary sign, according to the order which had been given to her about it. This spirit, I say, as white inside as it appears in countenance and clothing, leaving aside the black chalk, which it was claimed it would use to mark a sign of the cross on the white paper, takes the white chalk and without difficulty forms a cross on the upper part of the crucifix, the cross of which is made of Brazilian wood, wood strong and hard, and which, because of its hardness, cannot receive and retain the chalk even if it has been moistened. Several persons, the most qualified in the entire country, saw the said cross, and some among them tried to make a similar mark on the same wood and were not able to do it, which made them believe that it is not Huguette who did it, nor any man whatsoever, seeing that no one had entered the room since the spirit had been ordered to make the said cross until the Jesuit fathers entered, which was exactly at four o'clock in the morning,[37] at the same moment that the said spirit left after having said to Huguette that it had made and left a mark such that it

[37]This phrase generally meant "in the fourth hour after daylight," not at 4 AM. The same method of referring to time is used for all the morning hours; therefore "three in the morning" means "in the third hour after daylight."

would satisfy every Christian person who would see it or, without having seen it, would hear it spoken of.

Was not this mark sufficient in order to believe that this spirit was from God, a good and not an evil spirit? Yes, you say, if we were assured that the spirit had made it. So you do not believe that this cross is the work of the spirit? Let's discuss this topic a little and see if reason will be able to persuade you of the contrary. I speak to you who have seen the said cross and who still have its image imprinted in your imagination; two Jesuit fathers found this cross, which was not in existence at three hours and three-quarters in the morning, made when four o'clock sounded[38] that same morning. It was not in existence a quarter of an hour before, and now it is. Your eyes assure you of this truth. You would not dare say nor even think that it [the cross] was made by itself; therefore someone must have made it. It is not the two women who made it, to wit the sick woman and the lady Jeanne Massé, who alone was in the room, because in the judgment of the most reasonable men and according to what we have said above, she would not have been able to do it because of the wood. Besides, both of them were ready to swear in good faith that it was not made at three hours and three-quarters in the morning. It is not the Jesuit fathers who made it for the above reasons. They ought to be crucified if this were so. It is not, finally, little Claude, swaddled in his crib. It is, thus, no one of this world because no one else entered the room during that time. Therefore, we will judge that it is someone from the other world and assuredly a good spirit.

Here are my reasons. First, inasmuch as each thing is recognized in its like and as goblins and evil spirits are black, if this spirit of whom we speak had been one of these coalmen of hell, it would have chosen the black chalk rather than the white, which has always been the color of heavenly spirits and messengers of heaven, just as the color black has always been the mark of spirits of darkness. This is so evident that it does not need other proofs. The case posed that an evil and cursed spirit had taken the white chalk; being that it is the sworn enemy of the cross, it would not dare undertake to make this holy sign which it hates and flees more than one could imagine. But Satan, you will tell me, who oftentimes takes the shape of an angel of light in order to deceive and trick those who can be the most spiritual and the best informed, could, all black that he is,

---

[38]As in other early modern towns, Dole's residents kept time according to the sounding of church bells that rang approximately every hour. Only the more prosperous cities could afford the mechanical clocks that had been developed in the fifteenth century.

take the white chalk and, however much an enemy of the cross he may be, nevertheless make a more perfect and more accomplished cross than the one that had been made. In order to have done with these pretensions, I respond that it is true, and when men are such that they govern themselves by themselves, that they are prideful and presumptuous, God allows them to be humbled and exposed by their own enemy so that they may recognize their impoverishment and submit themselves henceforth to the pleasure of his divine majesty. Now what have you to fear here? It has been about forty days since this spirit made itself visible without giving the least sign of malice that one can think of. Besides, it appears to a woman so simple and so humble, so fearful and so obedient, that she cannot move away even the slightest bit from the order of her confessor, who after having communicated the affair to some learned and worthy persons, after having warmly recommended her to God in all possible ways, after having received from above[39] testimonies of the goodness of this spirit as evident, as very freely given, in confirmation of this truth, he will swing in the fire of hell when he is ordered to. And you will say after this that an evil spirit will have made this cross in order to seduce simple people obedient to God. Here is my third and unique reason, not making a big deal out of the two preceding ones. God, who rules us through men, will not allow us because of his love to be tricked in obeying them. Huguette takes counsel from her confessor on an affair as important as this one, by his order she asks this spirit for a sign of the cross as a testimony of its goodness, the cross was made in a better style than was expected, and therefore Huguette has not at all been deceived.

Now, the cross was made by a good spirit. God, who is always God and consequently always good, who spreads the grace of his divine providence over the wise in order to protect and defend them against their enemy....[40] The cross does not destroy itself. The cross was once planted on the mount of Calvary in order to save us, and this small, white cross was formed on another cross at the commandment of God by the above-named spirit in testimony that it is good, that it is true, and a spirit from God.

[39]This phrase can have a dual meaning. The various tests that the spirit was required to undergo were seen as tests of heavenly support of its visitations. As it is written, however, this phrase could also suggest that prominent people had come to support Huguette and her vision; it was part of the legal statutes in the Franche-Comté during this era that the testimony of an elite member of society (lawyer, noble, university professor) was more valid than that of a person with a lower social standing.

[40]The author seems to have lost track of the thread of his argument and does not complete this sentence.

Eighth Chapter

The thirty-seventh and thirty-eighth days. The spirit refuses to take the crucifix in its hand or the chalk in order to make the cross again in the presence of two Jesuit fathers and why.

 Here is the mark of this good spirit. You have seen it with your own eyes; now lend your ears in order to hear it speak, not by its mouth, but by that of Huguette, who alone receives in her ears the kinds of sound which it produces. And in order to understand the whole situation better, fix in your mind an image of the said Huguette, sick on her bed, and the neighbor woman, lady Jeanne Massey, on her knees, which she did for ten or twelve days in order to keep Huguette company when the spirit reassures her by its presence beside the bed.

See here a small table covered with a white cloth and on this a basin with holy water, a blessed lighted candle, a crucifix, an image of Our Lady of Montaigu, and a reliquary with the relics of the blessed father St. Ignatius, all adjoining the bed, and two Jesuit fathers, who wish to be on hand when the spirit arrives, from two hours after midnight on, waiting for it while praying to God. It comes in the same way as before, invisible to all save the sick woman who, by the order of the Jesuit father,[41] sprinkles it

---

[41] Although Mercier begins by noting that two Jesuits are with Huguette, for the rest of the chapter

with holy water and takes notice of its countenance, its face, and all the gestures of its body when she throws holy water on it and responds to the father that, without changing expression but rather bending down modestly, it bowed and at the same time made the sign of the cross on itself, raising its hand, white as snow, to its head, then to its belly, and from the far end of its left shoulder to its right, adding that this spirit had made the sign of the cross much better than she herself. The father orders it to kneel and to honor the relics which were on the table, to kiss the image of Our Lady, to worship the crucifix, to say prayers similar to those which we have already spoken about above, to make an act of contrition.[42]

Huguette replies that the spirit stepped back from the table to the middle of the room, while tucking up its gown a little in such a way that she saw its bare feet, which she desired to see for a long time. It kneeled and, joining its hands, extended its arms from its chest, stretching them in the air with the image of the blessed Virgin, beholding her with a smiling and devout eye, praying to her in this way: "Lady, Holy Virgin, excellent and very admirable mother, I acknowledge you as the mother of God, more eminent than all creatures whether of heaven or earth, and therefore I worship you with the honor of hyperdulia[43] as I worship your very dear son Jesus Christ, true God and true man, with respect and absolute sovereign honor. I honor you also as mother of mercy and the mediator of my salvation because by your means I overcame demons at the hour of death and have been preserved from the pains of hell."

In short, Huguette responds that the spirit did all that it had been ordered to, indeed more, because it kissed the said image again and again, that it seemed to desire to eat and swallow it, that it had beaten its chest while shedding tears in front of the crucifix, and that, at the end of all that, the said spirit had made the sign of the cross on itself. The father, neither seeing nor hearing anything except through Huguette's mouth, cannot content himself and be satisfied with that. This is why he proceeds and orders the spirit to take the crucifix on the table and to hold it in its hands. And as it apologizes, saying that it cannot do it, the father says to Huguette, "Tell the spirit that it can do [now] what it could the day before yesterday, and just as it took the crucifix from your hands to kiss it, worship it, and

---

he only mentions one.

[42]See note 25 above.

[43]The veneration properly given to the Virgin Mary, higher than *dulia*, the veneration properly given to saints and angels, and less than *latria*, the worship properly given to God alone.

make the little white cross on it, let it take it now so that we see it, or let it make again the cross that is half erased, otherwise we will believe that it's a lying spirit and you also."

So Huguette speaks thus to it by the order of the father, "Spirit, take this crucifix on behalf of God that at another time you worshipped with your hands and so devoutly. Take this chalk and make the cross again that you fashioned. Do it in the name of God; otherwise I renounce you as I renounce all the demons of hell and will believe that you are one of them! Do what I've told you quickly or leave this place in the name of God all powerful and the glorious prince of the angels, St. Michael, who chases all rebel spirits from paradise and threw them down into the deep pit of hell! Go there again, you, and may God confine you there!" And this said, she spits in its face two or three times.

These are, truthfully, very harsh and coarse words. These are coarse threats and spitting, shameful enough for a noble and generous spirit. Thus it does, indeed, show its generosity of spirit by both not becoming disturbed about this and not moving nor changing countenance the slightest bit, but beginning to speak again with more gentleness and sweetness than ever, it begins to draw a sigh from the depths of its[44] heart, crying out in a sad voice, "Alas, sweet Jesus, sweet Jesus, alas, where are we housed for the present? Oh, God, how incredulous the world is! I could indeed hold a crucifix in my hands because God wished it so and desiring that no one see it other than you, in whom one must believe being that you are not fantastic nor malicious, but I do not today what I could yesterday because God doesn't wish it. It is not his pleasure either that I refuse to make the cross that I made; he doesn't wish to satisfy the curiosity of those who are unwilling to believe anything unless they see it with their own eyes. They would like to see a crucifix in the air, held up by the hands of an invisible spirit, or else see a piece of chalk move while making a cross, at least the hand which moves it. And God is resolved not to do anything that they desire. If they are reasonable, let them be satisfied with reason without asking for miracles."

---

[44]In French, each noun has a distinct gender; for example, *esprit* (spirit) would have "he" as a personal pronoun, even if the spirit being written or spoken about was a woman. In "The History," Mercier's inconsistent use of nouns and their gender when describing the ghost heightens the story's tension and makes it harder to guess who the ghost might be. We have attempted to replicate this tension here, which is why we use "it" to refer to Leonarde here. Even though the spirit has been identified as Leonarde, Mercier wavers between "she" and "it" for personal pronouns referring to Leonarde.

The spirit, who was not free to stay in this world for as long as it would have liked and desired because it was at its best, suffering nothing, as it confessed, when it was traveling and it was doing its service, was ordered to withdraw and asks the sick woman if it should come tomorrow. She replies yes and the two days named above in order to complete its service of forty days according to the commandment that it had received from God. Upon this response, the end was prepared for, and the sick woman was made to make confession on that day in order to take communion the next day, which was the third Sunday after Easter, and to bless anew the room with ordinary prayers of the church.

The spirit does not fail to come at daybreak and, finding the sick woman alone, does its little bit of housework, makes her bed, sweeps the room, and puts everything in its place, and as the holy sacrament was brought a little late to give the said sick woman communion, the spirit did what it had not yet done, returning for the second time that morning and resweeping the room quickly in order better to honor Our Lord at the very holy sacrament of the altar.

Ninth Chapter

On the thirty-ninth day the spirit declares that it has spent seventeen years in purgatory, wherein is spoken of confession, communion, and devotion toward Our Lady.

 Monday [having] come and God having given to the spirit more power to manifest itself than before, it declared the reasons for which it had come back into this world and this in the presence of the Jesuit fathers who nevertheless did not hear it, but questioning it through the sick woman and through her received its answers, which I shall deduce here. Being therefore questioned if it was the same spirit who had come the thirty-eight preceding days, if it had made the small white cross, and if it confirmed everything that it says and does, it answers yes. It is asked, "Are you a pure spirit?"

"Yes, I am," it says. "Do not doubt this."

Huguette: "Are you a complete, spiritual substance?"

The spirit: "I don't understand the question that's being asked me."

"Are you a spirit who gave shape to a body in another time?"

"I'm a spirit who once gave life and movement to a body."

Huguette: "Where is this body?"

The spirit: "It's dispersed."

Huguette: "I'm asking where it was buried."

The spirit: "It was buried in the cemetery of the reverend father Franciscans."

Huguette: "In what spot?"

The spirit: "Near the cross."

Huguette: "On which side?"

The spirit: "On the side of the altar of Our Lady of the Angels."

Huguette: "A long time ago?"

The spirit: "Around seventeen years ago less three months."

"And this body which you have now, is it the one that you had while you were alive on earth?"

The spirit: "No, because it's dispersed and reduced to ashes, as I have already said."

Huguette: "What matter is it made of then, and where did you get it?"

The spirit: "I get it as God gives it to me when I come here. I am so comforted and pleased to be clad in it in order not to feel the fire of purgatory during this time that I pay no attention to the matter from which it is made."

Huguette: "Seeing that you speak to us of purgatory, is that where you have made your home for seventeen years since you left your body? Or else if you have been elsewhere...."

The spirit: "It's there that I have been without a break save from the first day that I came here to see you in this room to visit you. It's there that I purged my sins, burning in a fire so strong and so penetrating that if you only saw it you would be transfixed and you would die of fright and apprehension."

Huguette: "Good God! Seventeen years in a scorching fire! What would I do if I saw it, seeing that, hearing you speak, I'm transfixed! I'm speechless! I'm dying! Can God indeed, who is so merciful, see with his paternal eyes his poor children whom he destines for the inheritance of heaven fried for so long on these burning coals without some refreshment?"

The spirit: "In truth, our torments are so great that they can't be explained by us ourselves who experience them, but the mercy of God shines and glistens toward us in such a way that among these burnings and these fires neither the angels nor the archangels nor the cherubim, not even the highest spirits of paradise, would be able to comprehend it. It's true that we don't suffer in proportion to our faults, and therefore we praise and bless this merciful goodness though groaning more loudly than the three children in the furnace of Babylon ever did."[45]

---

[45]The legend of the three children of Babylon is based on a distortion of Daniel 4. In the biblical

Huguette: "May I be so bold as to ask you why this good God has kept you for so long plunged in these searing flames?"

The spirit: "Seeing that God allows me to say it, indeed orders me to, for my humiliation and for his glory, I will say it, and God wishes that those men and women who hear it make good use of it. The reason that I spent seventeen years in purgatory is that I made my confessions badly, saying my sins in general instead of declaring them in detail. For example, I accused myself of not having loved my God above all things and didn't declare what I had loved more than him, ignoring his holy commandments in order to do my will. And I accused myself generally of not having loved my neighbor as myself without making any other effort to examine in what way I had failed, if I had misjudged him in an important matter, how many times if I had reviled and slandered him, or if I had done him some wrong or injury, I accused myself in general of becoming impatient and angered and didn't say that, through impatience, I had said outrageous words, reproachful words, that I had cursed, slandered, and uttered other oaths. At other times, instead of humiliating myself by declaring my fault such as it was, I placed it on others, saying my mistress or my neighbor is so irksome, so mean, so terrible that she made me swear. I usually accused myself of my faults without understanding them well and weighing their gravity, inasmuch as they were made against such a good God, who had given me such easy and useful commandments to observe. Shamelessly I often repeated the same faults in my confession without mending my ways, mocking God, because I would promise the confessor, his lieutenant, to correct myself, and upon leaving confession I didn't think anymore about it. If some confessor reproved me for my faults or else advised me to do some good work, I didn't pay much attention to it, and sometimes I went looking for another confessor who told me nothing at all and who, after my confession, did not put my sins before my eyes again in order to make me feel ashamed and to humiliate me, of which I had great need as a very effective means to correct myself. In short, I

account, the Babylonian king Nebuchadnezzar orders a golden statue made and commands all residents of his lands to fall down and worship this statue when they hear any music. Three Jewish patriarchs do not and are thrust into a fiery furnace as their punishment. Because God blesses these patriarchs, they escape from the fire unsinged, which causes Nebuchadnezzar to decree that any who speak evil of the patriarchs' God will be killed. By the seventeenth century, this legend had been modified and enjoyed a venerable status in iconography and in sermons. The three patriarchs had become three children who suffered for God in the fiery furnace but eventually emerged unscathed. The image conveyed a powerful message about the extent to which a Christian should be willing to suffer for God and was frequently coupled with images that were metaphors for salvation.

hardly knew what it was to be sorry to have offended God, to detest one's sins, to cry over them, and to make a good penance for them.

I was also negligent in my communions, not having taken the necessary precautions, which don't merely consist of making confession well, but of considering who it is that one must receive, that it is Jesus Christ, God and man, in order to make us like him. I didn't consider that my Savior, whom I was going to receive in the very holy sacrament, was worshipped and revered by the angels. I should have kept them company without letting myself be distracted by contemplating something useless, and I should have fixed the eyes of my thought on the patience of my Savior, who in all the affronts which were made to him—stripping his clothes from him, flaying him with scourges, crowning him with thorns, calling him drunkard, Samaritan, and crucifying him ignominiously—never complained, never cursed anyone, but rather forgave and prayed for the evildoers. I would have made myself like him and would have become more patient than I was, and I wouldn't have been ashamed to pray to God in general every morning and when getting up [in the morning] in the presence of people, if I had considered that my Savior whom I was going to receive prayed for me on the mount of Calvary in the presence of more than 20,000, both Jews and Gentiles. When I was taking communion, I put all my devotion into saying Our Fathers and rosaries without attentively thinking about the death and passion of Jesus Christ, which he nevertheless desires to be diligently considered by those men and women who approached this precious sacrament, from which it happened that I didn't make much profit from my communions. These are those faults of mine that God ordered me to declare and for which I suffered so many pains, less though than the punishment owed for the sins committed."[46]

Huguette: "If you were negligent in your ordinary confessions, the last which you made, wasn't it accompanied by all the circumstances due to this very holy and august sacrament?"

The spirit: "Good God, how difficult it is to do well at the moment of your death something which you've never done well in your life! Alas, how God showed himself good toward me at that hour when giving me the desire to make confession with a regret for having offended him. For I could hardly say two or three of my faults, with a desire to declare all the rest, when violent coughing suffocated me, took away my speech and all

[46]This phrase intentionally invokes a conventual relationship between God and the sinner much like that between a subject and sovereign.

consciousness. Upon which, having received sacramental absolution, I left this world to descend to purgatory and would have descended to hell if the blessed mother of my God had not been my good advocate. Undoubtedly she kept me from dying on the road, carried in a cart where I was thoroughly shaken, and I don't know how I didn't die one hundred times before arriving in the city. This Lady granted me contrition for my sins; she negotiated my peace and reconciliation with her very dear son Jesus, whom I had so greatly annoyed by my sins. Dare I say that it was she who gave warning and had the priest advised to hurry to come quickly to absolve me of my sins. Holy Virgin, Blessed Virgin, refuge of sinful souls, be blessed forever! I owe you my life. Let it be soon that I see you in heaven in order to devote to you for all eternity the life which I hope to live there."

Huguette: "In order to have received favor from this Holy Lady, you must have shown her some extraordinary devotion. You did, I'm assured of it, some great thing in her honor. We have learned that you fasted on the eve of her triumphant assumption into heaven[47] while working in the harvest, eating nothing else but some fruit and drinking some water. You also fasted other eves and Saturdays dedicated to her name. You presented to her every day a beautiful wreath woven with sixty-three Hail Marys as so many beautiful roses in memory of the sixty-three years which she lived on earth.[48] Those of your acquaintance told us that about you, but they don't know everything. Tell us the rest in your words so that following your example we may make ourselves worthy of the protection of this empress of the world and her true servants."

The spirit: "Besides that stated above and other devotions which I can presently say, I had the custom of presenting to her every day five Our Fathers and five Hail Marys, imploring her and begging her by the five wounds of her well-loved son and by the sufferings which she felt standing at the foot of the cross at the hour of his death that she help me throughout my life and that she not abandon me in this last and so dangerous passage, where the bravest and the greatest saints tremble with fright. I had also vowed three pilgrimages in her honor which I didn't fulfill, but I'll tell you in another visit what must be done to free me from returning. Goodbye for now."

[47]14 August.

[48]In this case, the prayer Hail Mary is being treated metaphorically as a fragrant rose, a metaphor often used to refer to the Virgin Mary herself and which Mercier's reading of Leonarde's name in the final chapter will echo.

Tenth Chapter

On the thirty-ninth day for the second time it says it is the true aunt of Huguette, says something about its guardian angel, and asks for three trips to three places where Our Lady is honored.

 Having therefore returned the same day, always in the same way and more careful to do its housework well, the spirit says to the sick woman, "Now I have permission from God to tell you openly who I am and why I have come. I am your aunt, your mother's sister."

"My aunt," says Huguette, "was blind in one eye, and you have two eyes that can see clearly, which makes me think that you want to trick me."

To which the spirit responds, "This body that I have isn't the body that I once had, just as I've said, but it's one that God gives me, and he doesn't wish it to be defective because these bodies are whole. And if I appear younger, rosier, and whiter both in my body and my clothing than I was before my death, it's in order to make you realize that when we are resurrected on the great Day of Judgment, reassuming our true bodies which will have been as if reduced to nothing, we will not be old nor wrinkled, nor blind in one eye, hunchbacked or badly made, but young, well proportioned, and without any defects."

"Permit me," replied Huguette, "to ask you one more thing and tell me if it's true. Those who knew you and saw you more familiarly say that you had a ferocious way of speaking, abrupt and unassured, when you let yourself be controlled by your natural inclination. And now you are so gentle, so friendly, that often when I lost my temper and talking with you I called you a liar, a devil from hell to your face, you were not at all troubled or did not alter the slightest bit; rather you answered me like an angel from heaven. That's what astonishes me."

"They told you the truth," says the soul. "Only half blessed, I was sometimes ungracious and surly in my words, and it's in part the reason that I burned for so long in the fires of purgatory, as my guardian angel has informed me oftentimes when, being visited by it, I expounded on the unspeakable heat and mortal anguish of my heart, testifying to it an unequaled desire to leave these flames. 'Leonarde,' it used to say to me, 'Leonarde, my dear friend, I have great compassion for you and wish to free you from the pains which you suffer, but remember one must pay God down to the last penny for a single abrupt word that is the slightest bit repugnant to charity. You would not be able to enter into paradise without beforehand being purged in the purgative fire. If you had believed me when I said inwardly don't speak now, speak more softly or else mend your ways, or else correct yourself, you would have with little effort avoided these long, grievous torments. Nevertheless, take courage because here is Jesus Christ our redeemer, who seated at the right hand of his father represents to him the magnanimity with which he dealt with men, suffering their faults. He [Christ] offers him [God] his gentleness and his good-naturedness in order to deliver him from your impatience and from the pains that you suffer for this. Courage, have courage. The time of your deliverance approaches.' And thus this good guardian angel, still beside me at the present time, used to console me. Huguette, my friend, I would have a rough tongue and soul, but the fire in seventeen years has really smoothed them for me. This fire has, my God, made me as gentle as you see. Whoever wishes to follow the gentle lamb Jesus Christ into heaven must be gentle as he is."

Speaking of purgatory, Huguette asks if there was news down there of a certain young lady called Françoise Fauche, for she was most devout and all involved in God. She responded that not long ago the said young lady died, which was true, and that she had not been seen in purgatory. After that she says to Huguette, "I beg you not to question me any more because my time is short, and in the name of God listen to the reasons

why I have already visited you for thirty-nine days. Tomorrow, the fortieth, will be the last of my service, not, however, that I won't come to visit
you afterwards and will not fail in this until you have accomplished that
which I come to request of you and beg of you. God sent me here for three
specific things: firstly, to comfort you in your sickness, serving you as a
chambermaid and as a nurse, as a surgeon, healing you of a most serious
aneurysm or else of an illness which put you in danger of being crippled in
the left arm, and as a doctor who cures your pleurisy and continuous fever
which, having become a daily one, still persists, but it will be over soon.
Secondly, I came for the good of your little Claude, who would have been
without baptism or last name if God, using my hand with which I touched
you three times on the belly, had not taken pity on him and you; he or you
ought to have died or else both of you because of the great illnesses that
you had. I came also to teach you not to cover this child so much, often
having shown you how his coverlet needed to be turned back onto the top
of the cradle to give him a little air and some refreshment. That's why as
thanksgiving for all these good things received by the order of God and for
the easing of my pain three days from now, which will be next Thursday,
the first day of your leaving the house, you will go to the most reverend
father Franciscans to have a mass said at Our Lady of the Angels, which is
the privileged altar. Finally, I came for my own special interest in order
that you complete three trips that I ought to have made before my death,
which you will make in this fashion: you will go in the first place to Our
Lady of Montaigu which is at Gray, having your little Claude carried there
with you. You will go there with such company as pleases you, and as for
me I will never abandon you. You will see me always at your side or else in
front of you to clear the path for you. You will make this first trip like the
two others, living from alms, and upon passing through Pesmes you will
entreat the most reverend father Capuchins[49] to say two masses for me,
which they will very willingly do, on Saturday or on Monday to lessen the
pain of a poor soul of purgatory. It isn't necessary for you to attend nor
hear the said masses, but you can certainly hear the two which will be said
in Our Lady of Gray. The most reverend father Capuchins of that place,
who are charitable to all, will say them very willingly if you entreat them
to. That's all for the first trip."

[49]The Capuchins are a reformed branch of the Observant Franciscans, committed to following
the original guidelines of the Franciscan order as strictly as possible. They developed in the 1520s and
would become one of the more influential orders of reformed Catholicism in early modern Europe.

Our Lady of Montaigu. Engraving of the statue on display in the Capuchin church in Dole. The statue is 5.5 inches tall (close to the size depicted here). Image from Jean-François-Marie de Montépin, *Histoire abrégée des merveilles opérées dans la sainte chapelle de Notre-Dame de Gray* (Gray: F. Couan, 1757).

[Huguette]: "Before you move on to the other two pilgrimages, linger over this one awhile; examine well what you have just said. To speak clearly, I believe that you have told a lie. You have been dead for seventeen years; do you say that before you died you made a vow? And how would you have made this vow seeing that this devotion [to Our Lady of Montaigu] came seven or eight years after your death?"

The spirit: "May God prevent me from lying. I cherish the truth everywhere. You must know, then, that some time before my death God caused the great miracle at Montaigu in Flanders[50] in honor of the Holy

---

[50]Mercier here has made a geographical error; Montaigu is in Brabant, not Flanders.

Virgin. The miracles which happened were told so often with admiration down here that many from these neighborhoods went there themselves because of their devotion to this lady. I saw myself free, all alone; my mistress is in good enough health. I judged that I could indeed still make the said trip and contribute something of my own to the honor that was being paid to the queen of the angels and of men and on this made a firm resolution to make my way there. Not being able to accomplish this because of death, which surprised me, God willed me to speak to you so that you fulfill it in my place. Yet he doesn't oblige you to go so far as Montaigu but is satisfied on account of your indisposition, of the subjection to your husband, and other household hindrances, that you go to Our Lady of Montaigu who is honored at Gray. Don't find this strange because if priests and pastors of the church can dispense a person from vows for a legitimate reason, with even better reason God, to whom all vows are addressed, will be able to dispense a person from them. He assuredly dispenses me from them. And don't begrudge the steps and the person that you will take for me[51] because you won't lose anything in this."

Huguette: "I would be very content to make this trip, not only on your behalf but, in addition, for a vow that master Antoine, my husband, made because, seeing me at the point of death and fearing that the fruit that I was carrying and I should die, he vowed both of us to this beautiful lady. But we will fulfill our vow when we can. Because of my sickness, we aren't in a hurry. If it's necessary that we fulfill yours sooner, I am obliged to send someone there for you."

"It has to be you," responds the spirit, "who make this trip; otherwise it will be of no benefit. God has attached my deliverance from purgatory to this pilgrimage, made with the other two pilgrimages for us. Don't excuse yourself on account of your illness because God will heal you. Don't have any doubt about it. Tomorrow he will heal you. Trust in him and don't have any doubt about it at all. And therefore I beg you by the passion of Jesus Christ to agree to make this trip to Gray, after which you will go to Our Lady of Montjeux.[52] There's no need to carry your child so far, rather only to have a mass said by giving alms, which you will hear devoutly. This done, you will make your way to Our Lady of La Lève,

---

[51]Although the spirit here speaks in the singular, earlier it tells Huguette that more than one person can go on the pilgrimages with her. Later in "The History," it appears that at least several people go on each pilgrimage with Huguette, although they remain anonymous.

[52]The original text contains a mistranscription of Montaigu for Montjeux.

beyond Auxonne, under the same conditions as when you went to Our Lady of Mon[t]jeu[x] at such a sign that it should be a Saturday or Monday, because otherwise the masses will not be profitable to me. I will accompany you everywhere and will not leave you until the whole is completed, after which I will tell you the place where my good angel will lead me. God bless you, Huguette. Good-bye until tomorrow."

Eleventh Chapter

The spirit completes its services, asking pardon in case it has acquitted itself badly of its duty and promises to return. Prayers were said on this subject by the whole city.

 The next day, which should be the fortieth of the coming of the spirit and the last of its service, was a Tuesday, sixteenth of May, the day of St. Uval,[53] bishop who, among the graces which God had accorded him, was greatly enlightened in order to know the spirits. He had admirable power over those who are evil and enemies of God and of men. This provided the occasion to have recourse to this blessed saint, begging him very affectionately to share with us the enlightenment he had to distinguish among spirits and not to allow us to be deceived in this one here, who, albeit that it had only given signs of its goodness, nevertheless, we were not going to trust it yet. This is why recourse was had to prayers. This affair was commended unto all the monasteries and religious houses; my lords the canons and churchmen of Our Lady of Dole, by order of my lord the dean, as well as all those who have been informed about this spirit, pray to God to please declare its

---

[53]Most likely the twelfth-century Italian St. Ubald, bishop of Gubbio (d. 1168).

goodness through some irreproachable signs. In a word, some miracle was asked for which God did not grant, wishing that what had happened be considered attentively, as sufficient to make us put our trust in the said spirit, who came back on the fortieth day and left nothing to clean for the last time: made the bed, removed the spiders, swept the room, tidied up the hearth, put away the pots, ewers, saltcellar, and all the dishes on the buffet, hid the lamp that these good women held under the mantle in a chest. It scrubbed and wiped the table, benches, and chests so well that it seemed that everything was waxed they shined so much, to the great astonishment of those who saw it.

Afterwards, its housework done, doing reverence to the sick woman at its departure, it said to her, "Huguette, my good niece, my services are completed. What I have done is little compared to my goodwill, which is very large and affectionate toward the good and service of your person. Nevertheless, I did not acquit myself so well of my duty that I haven't made a lot of mistakes for which I beg compassion of God who commanded me to serve you. I also entreat you to pardon me for not having been served with the perfection that you could have wished for. Up until now you have seen me, sleeves pushed back, ready and dressed, in order to thrust deep into your bed and turn the straw upside down. Henceforth, you will see me with another bearing and countenance. In the past I came twice each day; from now on you will see me only once a day. Good-bye, Huguette, and take heart to begin the day after tomorrow your first trip to the church of the most reverend father Franciscans, where I will attend while you have mass said at Our Lady of the Angels."

"Don't come back anymore," says Huguette. "That's enough. I'm satisfied. If you visit me henceforth, I'll change houses. I'll go live somewhere else."

"So much the better," says the spirit. "Go wherever you please. You'll see me once every day until you have discharged that which I have required of you. Remember me often while saying your rosary, because I don't forget you in my prayers. Good-bye, my dear niece. God will be pleased to heal you as soon as I've left here."

Twelfth Chapter

On the forty-first day the spirit says not a word. On the forty-second it actively advocates that the trips it had asked for be completed.

On Tuesday, here is our spirit who comes in the early morning, not with sleeves pushed up like a chambermaid but with arms folded one on the other in the form of a cross, neither more nor less than those angels who are depicted on their knees contemplating the sad mysteries of the passion of Jesus Christ. It presents itself at the foot of the bed, standing upright, its eyes lowered, its head leaning a little toward its right shoulder without saying a word. The sick woman, or rather Huguette without a fever, is completely astonished and does not know what to say either. And after they look at one another for around the space of two Misereres,[54] the spirit, bending its head down and raising its hands in order to give the benediction over the bed, leaves. Huguette having explained what had happened that very morning, it is found good to have one of her friends come to be by her side, she about whom we have spoken above.[55] She [the neighbor] did that

[54]Depending on how quickly they spoke, it would take them approximately five to ten minutes to recite this prayer twice.

[55]Here Mercier probably alludes to Jeanne Masle, Huguette's neighbor who has appeared in several episodes of "The History" and who will be present at its culmination.

from then onward until the spirit's departure and was always present when it arrived.

The following Monday the said spirit returned with the same posture as the preceding day, without saying a word, and Huguette also lost her speech, but the friend, more daring, put her heart in her stomach and speech in her mouth and said to her, "You're holding a crucifix. Give it to the spirit to kiss. Ask it why it says not a word."

Now Huguette does it, and the spirit kisses the crucifix again and again, responds that it no longer speaks because it has said everything that it had to say and only waits for the execution of the trips which it had asked for. "Because today," says this good spirit, "you must begin. The fever is over. The trip isn't long. It's only three steps from here to the most reverend father Franciscans. Alas, my dear friend. Huguette, my good niece, have compassion for your poor aunt. If you knew what I am suffering outside of here, if you knew, you would go running to this privileged altar; you would have the precious blood of my savior Jesus offered to the eternal Father in order to refresh me from my torments."

Huguette: "Your words are so sorrowful that they disturb my whole heart, stir my entrails, and make tears flow freely from my eyes, but, alas, where do you want me to go all indisposed as I am, having forbidden me, anyway, from doing anything about that which you've required of me? On the one hand, I have compassion for you, but on the other, I do not wish to disobey those who have the power to command me."

The spirit, extending its hand, says, "Touch me, Huguette."

"I will definitely refrain from doing that," says Huguette, and the fear that she had was so great that she first thrust her arm back in the bed before she opened her mouth to speak.

The spirit replied, "Huguette, you do not have any fever. You're cured. What are you afraid of? Get up boldly and run quickly to this holy water that runs from the sacred side of Jesus Christ so that you extinguish the pitiless flames that burn me." Joining its hands and folding its fingers most firmly it says, "I beseech you by the five wounds of Jesus Christ your savior and mine, by the Holy Virgin Mary, the consolation of the afflicted, and in the name of all the saints, your advocates and mine, that you have to begin these trips, seeing that the fever has gone away."

[Huguette]: "But it's God who through his great power has chased it away. It's he who healed it."

The spirit: "It is God in truth who has returned you to health, but know that I pray very affectionately for it again and again so that without delaying any longer you would undertake the said trips." That said, it disappears. However, my lord the doctor visits her who was thought still to be sick and finds her pulse even and strong, in short, the pulse of a healthy person who can set off on a trip. Yet she did not leave the house that day nor the next either. Thus it was decided to summon this spirit, which was done in the following manner.

Thirteenth Chapter

By the order of my lord the dean, the holy sacrament is brought to the place of the spirit and it does not respond, being summoned.

 My lord the dean orders his two vicars to take themselves to Huguette's house with the holy sacrament, which they do at three o'clock in the morning, accompanied by two other churchmen dressed in their vestments. There are seven churchmen in the said house including the two Jesuit fathers. Huguette makes confession and takes communion, and the canticle[56] "Benedicte omnia opera domini domino" having been recited, the spirit appears in its customary way, invisible to all save to Huguette who indicated the place where it was. My lord the vicar asked it if there was someone in the room who had power and authority over it.

It replies through Huguette, "Indeed you know this. It is the true son of God and true man altogether who is truly in this most sacred sacrament of the Eucharist and would wish that you had eyes to see how I prostrate myself before his divine majesty, worshipping him with a supreme interior and exterior honor."

At the same time, Huguette saw the spirit on its knees, hands joined, worshipping him with external signs of a very great devotion. And as my

[56] A psalm or Bible passage chanted in church services.

lord the vicar had taken the ciborium[57] with the holy sacrament from on top of the table in order to hold it in the air in the place where the spirit appeared, Huguette saw the spirit bend down beneath it by however much the ciborium was lowered, and as the ciborium was so lowered that it was hardly farther away from the floor than half a foot, the spirit, always bending down beneath it, was so crouched and stuck against the paving stone that Huguette almost lost sight of it. It lets it be known by this submission and humility that it told the truth and that it knew its God, its savior, and its redeemer to be in the room. Nevertheless, it was not believed to be a good spirit, because all the demons of hell, whether they like it or not, bend the knee before this majesty. However, my lord the vicar goes even further and asks it if it does not recognize the power and authority that this same savior left in his church, if the priests of the Catholic, apostolic, and Roman church do not have the same power over all the spirits of the other world, to wit, of purgatory and of hell.

"They do not have the power over us who are in purgatory," says the spirit, "if God does not give them a particular privilege."

Huguette asks it if it will not respond to my lord the vicar by virtue of the authority that he has in the church. And it indicates no. Upon hearing this, my lord the vicar says, "I will see if you won't answer, O spirit, whatever you are, but before I speak I am going to confer with my God and prostrate myself before him in this precious sacrament."

Being therefore on his knees, he prays in the following way: "My savior, my lord, and my God, first sovereign priest on whom depends all the power that we have in the Church, I believe that all your words are completely true, you being the first and infallible truth. You assured us that all that we might ask you in your name should be granted to us. Well now, I beg you now for your greater glory and the edification of your Church that it please you to open the mouth and loosen the tongue of this spirit, likewise that it tells us who it is by irrevocable signs that may convince the most disbelieving. Oh, Lord of mercy, do not refuse us in a request that seems to us so just, where it is a matter of your honor and the good of your elect. Almost no one wishes to give credence to all that has happened here up to the present hour.

"Lord, here is the faith which goes away, half lost. It is almost extinguished. A large part of the world does not believe that there are spirits,

---

[57]The container in which consecrated hosts are kept and carried.

that our souls are immortal. So brutal and so carnal are we nowadays that some say it in words and many confirm it by deeds, because the care of the majority of mortals is to nourish and caress the body, to neglect their souls as if they were physical and corruptible even as are those of the brute beasts. If there is some vice which reigns in this city or in all of Burgundy by which your sovereign majesty is gravely offended and from which I desired that we reform ourselves, I pray you, make this spirit speak so that we may hear its voice. If you do us this favor, I vow in your presence to do such mortification as will be very agreeable to you. We will make sure that the word of this spirit will spread not only throughout this whole county and throughout all of the surrounding places, but also to the Indies, to Peru, to Brazil, to Japan, to China, and throughout the farthest confines of the earth. It seems, oh great God, that you are angry with us because the poor grape and pitiful grain harvests that we have had these last three or four years make us see that you have taken your hand away and locked up in the heavens your blessings that at other times you used to pour out liberally on the earth. Our sins, our ingratitude, our swearing, our curses which are so frequent in our mouth will have undoubtedly irritated you and given your majesty reason to punish us. If it is thus, oh God, make us know it through this spirit, that it speak intelligibly to us, and we will satisfy your divine justice. Penance will be published, and we will mend our ways.

"Oh God, Lord, order it to say what you wish us to do in order to advance ourselves in your holy service. Let it tell us that the honor that we bear you in this very admirable sacrament is agreeable to you, and we will increase it; if the frequent communions are made with a purpose that is suitable or not, and we will see to it. Let this spirit, who claims to be devoted to your holy wounds, declare to us by some words the great pleasure that we give you when we examine attentively the pains that you have suffered, and we will meditate on them. Trusting in your goodness, let me be so bold as to beseech it in your name.[58] I swear to you, therefore, oh spirit, whatever you are, I entreat you on behalf of my God and savior who is present in this very worshipful sacrament that you must tell me if you are here on behalf of God."

---

[58]The phrase, "en votre nom," can be translated with two meanings. The first is that given here where the priest invokes the power of God's name. The second has the sense of "in your behalf," so that the priest is asking this in the name of God, an action that in this circumstance is an extension of the priestly role.

The spirit is mute. It is begged two or three times to speak. It is questioned. The spirit is mute. It is questioned through Huguette if it comes in the name of the Father, the Son, and the Holy Spirit. It responds to her that it comes in the name of God. It is ordered once again to say distinctly if it comes in the name of the Father, the Son, and the Holy Spirit, and it responds for the second time, asking whether it is not enough that it comes in the name of God who does not permit it to say any more. Someone of the company wished to suggest other questions to this good woman in order, through her, to have the spirit's answer, but it was in vain; it kept silent just as it had promised. In fact, later it responded before its departure that God was greatly angered by the fact that they were importuning him too much, desiring miracles where there was no need of them.

"If one considers attentively," it says, "everything that happened in forty-three days and if one wants to follow the light of right reason without giving place to his imagination and to his own judgment, one will find out that I am such as I have declared myself, that is to say, a spirit from God, a reasonable soul, Leonarde Colin, your aunt who is in purgatory expiating my sins, waiting to be found worthy of heaven. And should there be no other proof than the cross that I made—God ordering me thus to do it in order to satisfy the desires of your confessor whom you can make no mistake in obeying, according to God—adding to this your health which I would dare to call a miracle, one must be satisfied. God knows well why he didn't allow me to say or do all that was desired of me. You know how many times you beseeched me to say my name, only I was not able to say it until the hour determined by this sovereign Lord. Undoubtedly I would have said it from the first day, indeed even from the first instant that I entered within, if I had had the power to, and at the same time I would have asked for the trips and the holy sacrifices of the mass that I have had permission to ask for the last four or five days. At least I would have entreated you to have some masses said, to have God prayed to for me, waiting for the fulfillment of all that I have asked you. I didn't have the power to ask for other suffrages. What would you do where God is the master and will be forever? His holy will is in everything and everywhere. Huguette, if I had accomplished it as I ought to do and could do, if in saying my Our Father I had attentively considered the words of the third petition while asking that your will, oh my God, my

Father, be done on earth by me and by all men as it is in heaven by angels and blessed spirits,[59] so many people would not have taken so much trouble for me, and me, the first, I would have been exempt from so many and such excessive torments that my disobedience alone to divine will caused me while I lived on earth and the space of seventeen years in purgatory from which you can pluck me by obedience! Huguette, my dear niece, God commands you to make the said trips for my deliverance. Make them then, and he will bless you. The benediction of the Father, the Son, and the Holy Spirit be with you."

The spirit, having made the above speech, heard by Huguette alone, disappeared, and my lord the vicar, accompanied by the other lords of the Church, brought the holy sacrament back into the church. God, however, who did not wish to give other public signs of this spirit, began to enlighten the understanding, to touch secretly the hearts, and to stir the affections in several ways of those who had become resolved against the spirit, disavowing everything that had been said or done by it. Certain others think about this spirit, feeling an extraordinary sweetness from paradise flow in their souls, which transports them out of themselves. Others also are so enlightened in the secrecy of their knowledge, so detest the abomination of their sins, that never had they seen themselves in such a state, both on the inside and on the outside, and so resolved to do good. Among others, the said Huguette's confessor had in his particular case some signs so evident that he cannot say when he will be ordered to put his hand in the fire in order to prove that this spirit is a soul from purgatory and a spirit from God but, nevertheless, that he is ready to do so.

---

[59]Here Leonarde paraphrases the prayer: "Our Father, who art in heaven, hallowed be thy name. Thy kingdom come, thy will be done, on earth as it is in heaven. Give us this day our daily bread, and forgive us our trespasses, as we forgive those who trespass against us, and lead us not into temptation but deliver us from evil. For the kingdom, the power, and the glory are yours now and forever. Amen." The "third petition" to which Leonarde refers is "lead us not into temptation but deliver us from evil."

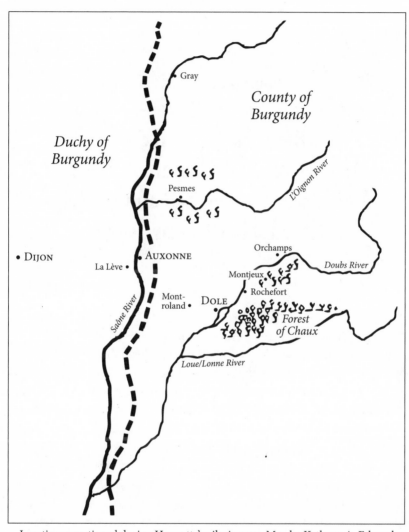

Locations mentioned during Huguette's pilgrimages. Map by Kathryn A. Edwards.

Fourteenth Chapter

From the forty-fourth day to the fiftieth the most reverend father Franciscans are visited and the trip to Our Lady of Gray is made.

 All of these signs, both internal and external being diligently examined, it is judged that Huguette was able to undertake the trips assigned by the spirit and that it would be an impious act and as a kind of cruelty if through a failure to accomplish them a poor soul was left to burn piteously who for a long time had been crying out for mercy and for help of those who could lessen its pains and who, moreover, were obliged to on the grounds of justice, having benefited under their relatives.[60] And although the said spirit had left them, the Saturday after the spirit's visit—more full of goodwill than ever—everyone makes preparations to go to the church of the most reverend father Franciscans. Little Claude is carried there, and masses are said at the altar of Our Lady of the Angels.

At one hour after noon on the same day, Huguette leaves Dole to go to Our Lady of Gray, although it was only three days after she had recovered from her fever after having borne it for forty-four days. She felt so strong that she outstripped in walking all the women and all the men who accompanied her, to their great astonishment. It is believable that the spirit

[60]That is, because Huguette and her mother received Leonarde Colin's small inheritance.

obtained for her by its prayers courage and strength from God, because it always walked in front of her, showing her a more cheerful face than usual, turning around sometimes, indicating the place where she ought to go. At other times she saw this spirit beside the child's cradle.[61]

She traveled four leagues[62] on foot, and after dinner Huguette arrived very early at Pesmes without being tired, as fresh, as little worn out as if she had not traveled. On Sunday, the most reverend father Capuchins of this place, entreated as much by the letters from their friars in the convent house of Dole as by Huguette and her husband, promised that although they were few, they would say two masses for the deliverance of this soul which was recommended to them. And not having been well informed about the days on which they ought to say the said masses, to wit, Saturday and Monday, they said one of them that very same day, which was Sunday, which was useful to the travelers because of the obligation that they had to hear mass that very day but was not profitable to the spirit, as we will see hereafter.

The mass finished, the trip was continued in order to arrive early at Gray [on Monday] and to arrange that the two masses could be said the next day, but before they had passed a small chapel, which is just before entering the woods of La Retie, the spirit, approaching Huguette, greets her courteously and apologizes that it had not visited her at four o'clock in the morning, as was its custom, since she was asleep and it did not wish to wake her. It asks how she was feeling on her trip, if she had been well received and housed at master Daniel Choublier's. Huguette responds that she had been so well received that she was surprised at the great charity which had been shown toward her.

"God be praised," responds the spirit. "He is powerful and good to repay abundantly the generosity of your host and hostess; they will lose nothing. Moreover, go at your own pace and don't walk so fast as you did yesterday. Nothing is pressing today. Besides, you can't ease my pain before the day of tomorrow. Nevertheless, warn these worthy people who accompany you to refrain from swearing and cursing because such things displease God greatly, being directly opposed to the second of his commandments, which is thou shalt not take the name of God in vain, nor anything similarly."

[61]This is a direct translation of the manuscript, although a *berceau* (cradle) would not be used while walking on pilgrimage. The author almost certainly means some kind of baby carrier.

[62]Approximately twenty miles.

And letting the men and the women of the company go ahead, it stopped beneath a tree where it showed her on a half-burned oak a beautiful woman holding a small chubby baby in her arms and a standard or a small banner, completely touching the child.[63] And both of them, to wit the spirit and Huguette, looked at this woman with so much pleasure that they could not move from there until the husband of the said Huguette, noticing that she was missing from the company, retraced his steps very hastily and found his wife at the foot of this tree, completely enraptured in contemplation of this admirable union. I leave you to think about what that can signify. We had absolutely no other knowledge of this which can be described on this paper.

The next day, which was Tuesday, the twenty-second of May, having made confession and being ready to take communion and hearing the two masses that the most reverend father Capuchins said before the altar of Our Lady of Montaigu for the purposes said above, Huguette saw the spirit standing upright beside the candlestick where the torch of the elevation was, sometimes on its knees at the foot of the altar and at other times as if jumping and springing about for joy like King David, who playing the harp used to jump in front of the ark of the Old Testament.[64] The devotion being finished, the host of our pilgrims, named Jean Georget, joined the most reverend father Capuchins so as not to return to the city, and some took the path to Dole and others that to [their homes in] Gray.

Now some hours after the said host had arrived at his lodging, he threw himself on the bed where, after having rested the slightest bit, here he sees himself raised from the ground with the bed and that three times. Really surprised, he calls out to the male and female servants and his wife. No one appears. From then on the bed is raised three times more and my man, still more surprised than before, raises his voice, yells, gets angry, and does not see anyone. He had not stopped speaking when he is lifted for the third time in the same way as before. And my host, completely afraid and indignant, throws himself suddenly from his bed, looks above, below, beside, and in the space between the wall and the bed, runs to the neighboring rooms, and does not see a living soul in the entire house, nor knew except through conjecture why this had happened: why, the spirit, most assuredly. We believe that it is it who raised the bed from the ground

[63]This apparition is like the vision that inspired the worship of Our Lady of Montaigu in Brabant and follows a common pattern in medieval popular visions.

[64]II Samuel 6.

because the day it took leave from Huguette to go to heaven, it said to her without inquiries being made about it and any news about it being known, "You will hear," it says, "through this young man of Gray, your host, what happened the day that you departed from there." When the spirit said this, the father-in-law of the young man, called Jacques Deniset, was at this place and in the room, who being asked if he did not know what the spirit meant, told the whole story that has been reported above. We learned about it since from the mouth of Jean Georget, to whom it happened.

The following Tuesday, the sky was troubled, the same night rain was feared, and the spirit came at two hours earlier in the morning than the other times, which assured good weather as it was also throughout the time of the three trips. The weather was so beautiful and so agreeable that one could not have desired more.

This spirit brought blessings where Huguette stayed because the wife of master Daniel Choublier, our pilgrims' host at Pesmes, going and returning from Gray, was sick, and she has been well ever since. Everyone is satisfied in this house; no one had good reason to wish not to have received such guests although they did not leave one single penny of silver there.[65] The spirit asked Huguette at the same time how she was feeling, and Huguette responded to it that she was feeling very well, thanks be to God, save for some small corns that she had on her feet. Fearing that they would prevent her from making her trip on foot, she asked it if returning home in another fashion [than on foot] would not diminish the merit of the trip. "No," it says, "my dear niece. God sees and is satisfied with your goodwill. Return home however you can." So she returned in a cart.

And as the spirit was still in the room, little Claude began to bawl, which he had done all night and about which Huguette complained, "Jesus, Mary, you wished me to drag this child on this trip, and all he does is cry all night preventing our good and charitable hosts from getting the slightest bit of rest! They were, in a manner of speaking, taken from their beds; they put us to bed in their rooms, and we have given them so much inconvenience that I'm ashamed of it."

"Patience," says the spirit. "If they have taken pains for you, you will have from it so much more merit. God will compensate all." Thus spoke this good-natured spirit, turning all the bad into good.

---

[65]To repay their host for the expenses he incurred.

I will say nothing about what happened from Tuesday evening until the following Saturday because we made the trip to Our Lady of Montjeux. You will learn, nevertheless, that the spirit, being questioned if the trip to Gray had been made according to its liking and if the masses had been said, responded that it was pleased about the first pilgrimage, save that only one mass had yet been said at Pesmes, which for not having been said on one of the two assigned days, its merit had not been applied to it [the spirit], which gave occasion to write to the most reverend father Capuchins of that place to ask if it was true that they had only said one mass for the soul in purgatory that had been recommended to them and this on Sunday. They responded that it was as the spirit had said and that they had not been able to satisfy the said masses, being that there were only two priests residing in their convent that whole time.

The spirit was asked in addition if one person in particular was doing some works for it. It responded that without a soul living on earth knowing it, "this person about whom you speak does nothing night and day other than pray for me and applies to me all the merit of the good works that he/she can do," a thing that was as true as it said. God manifested to it the good that was done for its deliverance.

Fifteenth Chapter

The trip to Our Lady of Montjeux is made and the fiftieth day of the apparition, the twenty-seventh of May.

 Saturday [having] arrived, the spirit appears in the early morning saying to Huguette, "My dear friend, if you had done what I promised you at the beginning, from the Thursday of the other week, without delaying until Saturday two days later, today would be my last visit, and I would bid you adieu to go off to fully enjoy in paradise the one who created me for this purpose and, being himself made man, died on the cross in order to clear the path [to paradise] for me. That which is not done at this time will be done Monday, God helping. Two days in purgatory will be very fiery and sorrowful for me, but I am resolved to suffer everything in order to satisfy divine justice and pray this infinite goodness to give so many graces to those who have prevented you from executing promptly the said trip that when leaving this world they be found so pure and clean that they have no need to be purged in the hot embers that have burned me for the space of seventeen years, but from this temporal life they enter straightaway into the glorious and immortal life. However, get up, Huguette, my friend. Take some holy water. Fortify yourself with the sign of the cross. Kneel in front of this crucifix and the images of the glorious Virgin Mary and St. Ignatius. Offer your trip to Montjeux to God. Before leaving the house, put your affairs in order; put your child in the care of some good female neighbors until your return, which will be around four o'clock in the evening. Tell your husband to go fetch a priest to celebrate mass. Carry in order to celebrate mass, carry pure wine in a small bottle for this purpose because you aren't assured of finding any; the hermit father will maybe have already said mass when you arrive. Do what I tell you, my good niece, and I'm going to wait for you near the God of Pity, which is beyond the Besançon gate. You'll find me there, and I'll accompany you without abandoning you."

Everything was executed point by point as much on Huguette's part as that of the spirit. This short trip is made joyfully and with devotion. Jesus, how beautiful it was to see five or six pilgrims of Our Lady of Montjeux singing litanies in the uncultivated fields and reciting their rosaries, and Huguette, with more consolation than all the others, always seeing before her her spirit who served her as a guide. If you had seen it, you would have taken it for the angel who was the guide of young Tobias,[66] but I do not know if I dare to say what happened passing on the bridge of Rochefort. No, I don't want to say it, nor will I therefore say that master Antoine Roget with one of his male neighbors, who kept him company, feared that the spirit that we have compared to Raphael, great friend of man, was some kind of demon, suspecting that it would push this woman in the water. "For," he said after several other things, "in all these three trips that the spirit asked for, we must cross three rivers. We have already crossed the Oignon going to Our Lady of Gray. Everything goes well on that score, thanks be to God, but there will be something to fear when we have to cross the Saône upon leaving Auxonne to go to Our Lady of La Lève. We must be afraid now also while crossing the Doubs on this wooden bridge without a railing that this spirit, whatever it might be, will be able indeed to commit some affront against you. Let's take heed there, and without other discussion, entering onto the said bridges, let's take Huguette by the arms and lead her to the end of this bridge."

But Huguette, knowing well their intentions, said to them, "Fie my friends, what are you thinking of? What are you afraid of? Would you really think that the spirit who negotiated my health with God when I was lying on my bed would now wish to push me down into the Doubs in order to rob me of my life which it gained for me with such care? If it had been a spirit such as you imagine, would it have waited so long to make

---

[66]From the book of Tobias in the Old Testament. Guided by the angel Raphael, who is disguised as a traveling companion, Tobias cured his father's blindness and expelled a demon from Sarah, the daughter of one of his father's kinsmen.

me feel the effects of its malice? Undoubtedly it would have strangled me more than one hundred times when I was all alone in my small room without putting off the execution of such an unhappy plan until the present. If it had given you at least some indication of wickedness, you would have occasion to doubt it and would be watchful for yourselves and for me, but, not having any fear while it goes in front of me, as it is doing now on this bridge, I believe that it's so unlikely that it wishes to harm me that, rather, if through some accident I were to fall into the river, it would pluck me out of it in order to lead me to this beautiful lady where we're going. Here we are at the end of the bridge. We're in a safe place. Let us banish all fear and put our trust in God. My good friend, my companion Jeanne, let's let these men go on ahead and resume our devotions in this beautiful field. Let's sing aloud the litanies of the glorious Virgin Mary."

The trip continues, the mass is said at Our Lady of Montjeux, the spirit attends it, and everyone returns from there with more blessings than when we had gone there.

Sixteenth Chapter

The trip to Our Lady of La Lève is made, and the spirit takes its leave and goes to heaven.

The next day, the day of Sunday, we set off to go sleep at Auxonne, and in the early morning Huguette, woken by the spirit, went to Our Lady of La Lève, accomplished her devotions, and was brought back by this one [the spirit] in good health and with the good weather. I say with the good weather because all Sunday morning it had rained, and it was feared that the rain would continue, but at one hour after noon, from the moment that Huguette left the house to travel, the good weather started again and continues so well that our pilgrims in all their three trips did not get a drop of rain.

Now it is time that we put an end to this narrative, seeing that the trips asked for by the spirit are completed and that this one [the spirit], in order to acquit itself of its promises, must end its visits, never to return again. Here, therefore, is the result of its appearances, so frequent, similar at the beginning and throughout their progress.

The first appearance and entrance of the spirit were very good. The second, third, and all others assured us of the holiness of this spirit who not having appeared in the evening, rather has appeared for the last thirteen days in the morning and once a day only to Huguette who had seen it all day long while traveling until four hours after noon and did not believe she would see it again that day until the morning of the following Tuesday.

But God did not wish this blessed soul, purged enough, to remain one moment more in purgatory than he had determined; having entirely satisfied divine justice through the order of the same God, the spirit comes at an extraordinary time, not however at an inappropriate hour, to thank its benefactress and declare the place where it was going, with the promise never to forget the good service which she had done for it.

A little after seven o'clock in the evening, when master Antoine Roget, Huguette's husband, was having a light meal with five or six of his friends, the said Huguette, being seated beside the fire with her small child swaddled, and her good friend Jeanne keeping her company, suddenly sees this spirit come to her, but more beautiful and more glowing and more gracious than she had seen it and than it had appeared in the past. Especially since she did not expect it at that time, she says frightened and all trembling in a low voice to her good friend, "Here's the spirit."

"Courage," says lady Jeanne. "What are you afraid of? Ask it bravely if you have faithfully accomplished and completed its trips, if something was omitted that it desires, and it will be done."

"Everything's fine," says the spirit. "I am satisfied, but you will hear the young man from Gray or your host talk about what happened to him the day that you left there."

Huguette did not know what the spirit meant by that, but master Jacques Denezet,[67] father-in-law of the young man, through a coincidence, recounted what we said above.

After this the spirit speaks and says to its liberator, "This is not all, my dear niece. If you took pains for me, it is reasonable that you be compensated for them. I thought when we made our trips together that you would say some word to me and that you would ask me for something which, however, you didn't do. But now think about what you desire from me, and I will spare no efforts with God in order to have you obtain everything you will ask me for."

Huguette, completely moved and seized with a reverential fear looking at this spirit brilliant as a sun and hearing that it was going to heaven to serve as her intercessor and so as to obtain for her everything that she would ask it for from God, quickly goes to her knees, as do those who were in the room, joining her hands and with tears in her eyes, opening her mouth, presents her request to this spirit from God: "Oh, blessed soul,

[67]The same Jacques Deniset mentioned previously.

Leonarde Colin, my dear aunt, why didn't I know from the first day that you paid me the honor to come visit me by serving me as if you had been my chambermaid, why didn't I know from the first day what I know now? Why didn't I know you for such that you were? Alas, if I had known you, I wouldn't have thought to treat you so inhumanely as I did! How many times did I call you a lying spirit? How many times did I spit in your face? How many times did I call you Satan, evil spirit, devil from hell? Oh, my good aunt, I beg you for mercy! Pardon me for so many affronts and such great crimes that I committed toward you. I didn't know you. Pardon me, please! But how will you pardon this ungrateful and unthoughtful creature? My father, Jean Roy, my mother, Blaise Colin,[68] and I, your ungrateful niece, enjoyed the fruit of your work, and we inherited the little money that you had. Yet for all that, we let you burn piteously seventeen years in purgatory, and I regret more the two last days that you stayed there than all the rest because it's my entire fault. If I had obeyed you, as I ought to do, if I had accomplished your trips last Saturday, from then you would have been out of pain; you would right now be glorious in heaven, or from that very time you would have done acts of God's love which would be worth more without comparison than all that is done in this world here below in the service of the same God. It is my fault, it's true, but please consider that it's not all mine and that, if I disobeyed you not knowing you, it was so as not to disobey those that I knew as the lieutenants of my God. And I acknowledge, my good aunt, the mistake that I made and ask for paradise for my husband and for this your little nephew, who owes his life to you, after owing it to God. Pray up there in heaven for my father confessor, for those who helped in my sickness, for my good friend who is here, and for those who are in this company. Don't forget those who prayed and had masses said for you and several who still doubt whether you are a good spirit. And when you are with God, entreat him as much as you can that it please him to show us by some clear signs that, from purgatory, you have been received and raised into glory."

"My dear niece," replies the spirit, "God may wish to pardon all the offenses that you have committed against the divine majesty. As for me, I don't count myself offended. It's I who ought to ask your pardon for having inconvenienced you so much and for such a long time as I did. And

---

[68]It was not common practice in the seventeenth century for women to take their husband's names when they were married, although their children would have the husband's last name.

because the inconvenience that I gave you results in my benefit and my consolation, I will be grateful to you in heaven where very assuredly I am going. I dare promise that you will come there with your husband and your child as you desire. I assure you that you will have me ceaselessly as an advocate with our great God so that he gives you ceaselessly his holy grace thanks to which you may arrive at the glory that you desire. As for your confessor, he recommended himself enough to me. I will not forget him, nor those who helped you and were of some service to you during your sickness. Those who prayed or had prayers said for me, with God's help, will feel the effects of my arrival in heaven. And not only those, but also those who reviled you and had a bad opinion of me. I will pray generally for all, because the perfect love which reigns above loves friends along with enemies. If it pleased God to declare that I am Leonarde Colin, your aunt, and that I am going to heaven by clearer signs than those that he ordered me to give in order better to establish this truth among those who don't believe easily, I would really desire it, but my heart tells me that he doesn't wish to do it. I will entreat him for it, however, for the great good that he can bring about throughout his whole church. I pray this great God who through his mercy pulled me from prison into freedom, from tears to joys, from torments to entertainments, from fires to refreshment, that it please him to give us his blessing. Adieu, Huguette. I will never see you again in this world here below, but really wish that we will rejoice together in heaven in order to forever bless him who invites me there. Now I see this beautiful paradise partly open, the saints prepare to come before me, and my God holds in his hands a beautiful garland of roses, a crown of precious stones and pearls with which he comes to crown me. During my life, I was a poor servant, and now he pays me the honor indeed to call me his wife. Come, he says, come, my dear spouse, because I wish to crown you. So good-bye, good-bye. I am going to paradise to be crowned there."

Seventeenth Chapter

Final conclusion, a prayer of congratulation by Huguette's confessor made on her crowning in heaven.

Oh, soul beloved of God, spouse of Jesus Christ, hardly did you stop talking on earth than you made your entry into heaven where, absorbed into the indescribable pleasures which are above, you forgot the travails of this life and the torments that you suffered in purgatory. When you needed our suffrages, you visited us, and now that you enjoy the sovereign good outside of which there is nothing to desire, you no longer come to visit us. If we are unworthy of your visits, being that our earth is unworthy of bearing a glorious spirit, at least look at us plunged into the misery of our sins and imperfections. We implore your aid just as you asked for and implored ours these past days. I beseech you by your riches and by the inexhaustible treasures which you enjoy in heaven that you obtain for me in this world the poverty of Jesus Christ. I pray you by the torrents of pleasures and satisfactions that ravish your heart that I have a good share in the sorrows and torments which this my savior endured and suffered for the love of me. I beg you by the crown of glory that he puts on your head that he makes me worthy of his crown of thorns and that I be from henceforth despised and mocked as I deserve to be. The true pleasures, honors, and treasures are in heaven. In order to obtain them I desire here below the poverty, sorrows, and contempt that Jesus Christ suffered. Obtain for me this favor from my God, for which I beg you and will not stop begging you all the days of my life, believing surely that you are in credit with God because I see that he crowns you as his dear and beloved. I should not have had the good fortune to be in that room that you sanctified by your presence when you left it never to return there anymore. Certainly it is true that I thought of you prostrated before my God in the holy sacrament of the altar, and while I was praying to this great God, observer of our battles, to have pity on you who had struggled and fought so long, enduring the fires and flames of purgatory, I heard an inner voice who told me, "Pray no more for her who you think to be among the battles; she is victorious over the fires and over all kinds of torments. Don't look for her any longer in the prisons and subterranean dungeons of purgatory, but raise your eyes to heaven, and you will see how God is crowning her." I believe that it is the good angel, your guide, who gave me intelligence of your glory and a little later made me think of your name in which I found what happened in heaven, you entering there glorious and triumphant. "Leonarde Colin," this good guardian angel said to me, "and God crowned her. It's all one. It's her anagram," reflecting on which I found that it was necessary only to change the first letter into a D.[69] And completely joyous as you were, completely deified, a small drop of water absorbed into an immense ocean of pleasures and satisfactions that are in God, I congratulated you as I could for the great good fortune that had happened to you, beseeching you at that time as I am doing now and will do all my life that you help me to make a good penance for my sins in this world so that upon leaving this one [world] pure and clean I can go to see you, bless, praise, know and love my God forever. Amen. The 24 July 1628.

[69]An anagram is a word play in which the letters of a word or a phrase are rearranged to form another word or phrase. Anagrams were a traditional part of hagiographies, where they were seen as foreshadowing the saint's fate, providing a window into God's intentions for those wise and pious enough to read them correctly. In Leonarde's case, Mercier's substitution leads to *Deonarde*, which broken into two becomes *deo* and *narde*. A *nard* or *nardum* was an herb with a particularly beautiful fragrance, so Leonarde's name suggests that she was a beautiful aroma sent from God.

Works Cited

MANUSCRIPTS AND ARCHIVAL SOURCES

Archives départementales du Doubs, series 2B549 and 2B2373.

Archives départementales du Doubs, series 10F42, 54, 56–65, and 69.

Archives départementales du Jura, series G78, G79, G82, and G96.

Archives municipales de Dole, 3, 78, 117, 400s, 639, 1474, and 1583.

Archives municipales de Dole, series GG9, GG12, GG15, GG21, and GG54.

Bibliothèque municipale de Besançon, Collection Chifflet, ms. 103.

Bibliothèque municipale de Dole, mss. 121, 126, 131.

Bousigue, Norbert. *La vie paroissiale à Dole au temps de la Contre-Réforme*. Mém. de maîtrise, Université de Dijon, 1989.

De Mesmay, Jean Tiburce. *Dictionnaire des anciens familles de la Franche-Comté*, 10 vols. Typescript. Bibliothèque municipale de Dole.

Tissot, M. "Notice sur l'établissement et les statuts de l'inquisition en Franche-Comté." Mémoire read at the Sorbonne in 1865. Typescript. Bibliothèque municipale de Dole.

TEXTS PRINTED BEFORE 1800

Boguet, Henry. *Discours exécrable des sorciers*. 2nd ed. Paris: D. Binet, 1603. Translated by Montague Summers as *An Examen of Witches* (London: John Rodker, 1929. Reprint, New York: Barnes & Noble, 1971).

Bona, Jean (Giovanni). *Traité du discernement des esprits*. Translated from the Italian by M. L. A. D. H. Paris: Louis Billaine, 1675.

Boyvin, Jean. *Relation fidèle du miracle du saint sacrement, arrivé à Faverney en 1608....* Edited by A. Guenard. Besançon: Othenin, Chalandre fils, 1839.

Cousin, Gilbert. *La Franche-Comté au milieu du XVIe siècle ou Description de la Haute-Bourgogne connue sous le nom de comté*. N.p., 1552/1562. Translated by Émile Monot (Lons-le-Saunier: L. Declume, 1907. Reprint, Lons-le-Saunier: Arts et littérature, 2000).

Geizkofler, Luc. *Mémoires de Luc Geizkofler, tyrolien (1550–1620)*. Translated by Edouard Fick. Geneva: Jules-Guillaume Fick, 1892.

Gollut, Loys. *Les mémoires historiques de la république séquanoise et des princes de la Franche-Comté de Bourgogne.* Dole: A. Dominique, 1592. Reprint, Roanne: Horvath, 1978.

Montépin, Jean-François-Marie de. *Histoire abrégée des merveilles opérées dans la sainte chapelle de Notre-Dame de Gray.* Gray: F. Couan, 1757.

Palafox, Jean (Juan) de. *Lumière aux vivans par l'expérience des morts, ou diverses apparitions des âmes du Purgatoire de nostre siècle, qui racontent leurs peines et en recherchent le soulagement auprès de la Vénérable seur Françoise du Très S. Sacrement.* Translated from the Spanish by Albert de St. Jacques. Lyon: Pierre Guillimin, 1675.

Petremand, Jean. *Recueil des ordonnances et edictz de la Franche-Comté de Bourgogne.* Dole: A. Dominique, 1619.

Regnault, Georges. *Les ordonnances anciennes, observées en la court souverain du Parlement de Dole et aux justices inferieurs du Comté de Bourgogne.* Lyon: 1540.

St. Jacques, Albert de. *La sainte solitude, ou les bonheurs de la vie solitaire, avec une description poétique du saint désert de Marlagne, prosche Namur.* Brussels: Goddefroy Schoevarts, 1644.

———. *La vie de la venerable mère Térèse de Iesus fondatrice des Carmelites de la Franche-Comté de Bourgogne.* Lyon: Mathieu Liberal, 1673.

Texts Printed after 1800

Ahlgren, Gillian. *Teresa of Avila and the Politics of Sanctity.* Ithaca, NY: Cornell University Press, 1996.

Apps, Lara, and Andrew Gow. *The Male Witch in Early Modern Europe.* Manchester, UK: Manchester University Press, 2003.

Ariès, Philippe. *Centuries of Childhood: A Social History of Family Life.* Translated by Robert Baldick. New York: Vintage, 1962.

Bavoux, François. "Loups-Garous de Franche-Comté: Identification du refuge et observations sur le cas de Gilles Garnier." *La nouvelle revue franc-comtoise* 1 (1954).

Beauquier, Charles. *Les mois en Franche-Comté: Croyances et coutumes populaires.* Barembach: J. P. Gyss, 1984.

Behringer, Wolfgang. *Witches and Witch-Hunts: A Global History.* New York: Polity Press, 2004.

Bienmiller, Daniel. "Dole et la mystique du cloître." *Mémoires de la société pour l'histoire du droit et des institutions des anciens pays bourguignons, comtois et romans* (1992): 53–64.

———. "Reflets de la Contre-Réforme: Le chapître de Dole et les visites pastorales." *La nouvelle revue franc-comtoise* 59 (1976): 157–67.

———. "Reflets de la Contre-Réforme: Dole et les dévotions populaires au lendemain du Concile de Trente." *La nouvelle revue franc-comtoise* 69 (1979): 33–42.

———, and Michelle Millet. *Univers folklorique et sorcellerie à Dole. Cahiers dolois* 1 (1977).

Bossy, John. *Christianity in the West, 1400–1700.* New York: Oxford University Press, 1985.

Brady, Thomas A., Jr. *Protestant Politics: Jacob Sturm (1489–1553) and the German Reformation.* Atlantic Highlands, NJ: Humanities Press, 1995.

———, Heiko A. Oberman, and James D. Tracy, eds., Handbook of European History, 1400–1600: Late Middle Ages, Renaissance, and Reformation. 2 vols. New York: E. J. Brill, 1994.

Briggs, Robin. *Communities of Belief: Cultural and Social Tension in Early Modern France.* New York: Oxford University Press, 1995.

———. *Witches and Neighbors: The Social and Cultural Context of European Witchcraft.* London: HarperCollins, 1996.

Brockliss, Laurence, and Colin Jones. *The Medical World of Early Modern France.* New York: Oxford University Press, 1997.

Brown, Peter. *The Body and Society: Men, Women, and Sexual Renunciation in Early Christianity.* New York: Columbia University Press, 1988.

———. *The Cult of the Saints: Its Rise and Function in Latin Christianity.* Chicago: University of Chicago Press, 1981.

———. *Society and the Holy in Late Antiquity.* Berkeley: University of California Press, 1982.

Bynum, Caroline Walker. *Jesus as Mother: Studies in the Spirituality of the High Middle Ages.* Berkeley: University of California Press, 1982.

———. *The Resurrection of the Body in Western Christianity, 200–1336.* New York: Columbia University Press, 1995.

Caciola, Nancy. *Discerning Spirits: Divine and Demonic Possession in the Middle Ages.* Ithaca, NY: Cornell University Press, 2003.

Chevalier, Bernard. *Les bonnes villes de France du XIVe au XVIe siècle.* Paris: Aubier Montaigne, 1982.

Clark, Stuart. *Thinking with Demons: The Idea of Witchcraft in Early Modern Europe.* New York: Oxford University Press, 1997.

Collins, James B. *The State in Early Modern Europe.* New York: Cambridge University Press, 1995.

Delattre, Pierre, ed. *Les établissements des Jésuites de France.* 5 vols. Enghien: Institut supérieur de théologie, 1949–57.

Delsalle, Paul. *Lexique pour l'étude de la Franche-Comté à l'époque des Habsbourg.* Besançon: Presses universitaires de Franche-Comté, 2004.

———. *Vivre en Franche-Comté au siècle d'Or, XVIe–XVIIe siècles.* Besançon: Cêtre, 2006.

Duchet-Suchaux, Monique, and Gaston Duchet-Suchaux. *Dictionnaire du français régional de Franche-Comté.* Paris: C. Bonneton, 1993.

Edwards, Kathryn A. *Families and Frontiers: Re-Creating Communities and Boundaries in the Early Modern Burgundies.* Boston: Brill, 2002.

Eire, Carlos M. N. *From Madrid to Purgatory: The Art and Craft of Dying in Sixteenth-Century Spain.* New York: Cambridge University Press, 1995.

L'Enfant Jésus, Sister Marie de. *Carmélites d'hier et d'aujourd'hui: D'Espagne en Franche-Comté.* Paris: Éditions Alsatia, 1967.

Farr, James. "Popular Religious Solidarity in Sixteenth-Century Dijon." *French Historical Studies* 14 (Fall 1985): 19–214.

Febvre, Lucien. *Notes et documents sur la Réforme et l'Inquisition en Franche-Comté.* Paris: Honoré Champion, 1912.

———. *Philippe II et la Franche-Comté.* Paris: Honoré Champion, 1911.

Ferry, Marcel. *Vierges comtoises: Le culte et les images de la Vierge en Franche-Comté en particulier dans le diocèse de Besançon.* Besançon: Cart. Editeur, 1946.

Feuvrier, Julien. *Le Collège de l'Arc à Dole.* Dole: Paul Chaligne, 1887.

Gay, J.-L. "Contribution aux origines du droit des gens mariés dans le Comté de Bourgogne." *Mémoires de la société pour l'histoire du droit et des institutions des anciens pays bourguignons, comtois et romans* 27 (1966): 197–220.

Gélis, Jacques. *A History of Childbirth: Fertility, Pregnancy, and Birth in Early Modern Europe.* Translated by Rosemary Morris. Boston: Polity Press, 1991.

Gresset, Maurice. "Dole et l'hostie de Faverney." *Mémoires de la société pour l'histoire du droit et des institutions des anciens pays bourguignons, comtois et romans* (1992): 65–78.

Hanley, Sarah. "Social Sites of Political Practice in France: Lawsuits, Civil Rights, and the Separation of Powers in domestic and State Government, 1500–1800." *American Historical Review* 102, no. 1 (1997): 27–52.

Headley, J. M. "The Conflict between Nobles and Magistrates in the Franche-Comté, 1508–1518." *Journal of Medieval and Renaissance Studies* 9, no. 1 (1979): 49–80.

Le Goff, Jacques. *The Birth of Purgatory.* Translated by Arthur Goldhammer. Chicago: University of Chicago Press, 1984.

Levack, Brian. *The Witch-Hunt in Early Modern Europe.* 3rd ed. New York: Longman, 2006.

MacDonald, Michael. *Mystical Bedlam: Madness, Anxiety and Healing in Seventeenth-Century England.* New York: Cambridge University Press, 1981.

Major, J. Russell. *From Renaissance Monarchy to Absolute Monarchy: French Kings, Nobles, and Estates.* Baltimore, MD: Johns Hopkins University Press, 1995.

McTavish, Lianne. *Childbirth and the Display of Authority in Early Modern France.* Brookfield, VT: Ashgate, 2005.

Monter, E. William. *Witchcraft in France and Switzerland.* Ithaca, NY: Cornell University Press, 1976.

O'Malley, John. *The First Jesuits.* Cambridge, MA: Harvard University Press, 1993.

Pidoux, A. *Une confrérie de cordonniers aux XVIe et XVIIe siècles: La confrérie de Saint Crépin de Dole, en Franche-Comté.* N.p.: Imp. Assoc. ouvrière de Bois-Colombes, 1910.

Pidoux de la Maduère, Sylvain. *Les officiers au souverain parlement de Dole et leurs familles.* 4 vols. Paris: Le Perreux, 1961.

Rance de Guiseuil, Charles. *Les chapelles de l'église de Notre-Dame de Dole.* Paris: A. Picard et fils, 1902.

Roper, Lyndal. *Oedipus and the Devil: Witchcraft, Religion, and Sexuality in Early Modern Europe.* New York: Routledge, 1994.

———. *Witch Craze. Terror and Fantasy in Baroque Germany.* New Haven, CT: Yale University Press, 2004

Rublack, Ulinka. *Reformation Europe.* New York: Cambridge University Press, 2005.

Sluhovsky, Moshe. *Believe Not Every Spirit: Possession, Mysticism, and Discernment in Early Modern Catholicism.* Chicago: University of Chicago Press, 2007.

Stone, Lawrence. *Family, Sex, and Marriage in England, 1500–1800.* Harmondsworth, UK: Penguin, 1977.

Surugue, René. *Les Archevêques de Besançon: Biographies et portraits: Histoire d'ensemble de la Franche-Comté; Histoire générale du diocèse et de la ville de Besançon.* Besançon: Jacques et Demontrond, 1931.

Theurot, Jacky, et al. *Histoire de Dole.* Roanne: Éditions Horvath, 1982.

Thiry-Duval, Hervé. *L'esprit féerique: Dictionnaire des fées en pays comté.* Langres: D. Guéniot, 2003.

Venard, Marc, ed. *Histoire du christianisme.* Vol. 8, *Le temps des confessions (1530–1620).* Paris: Desclée, 1992.

Walter, Hélène et al. *Histoire de la Franche-Comté.* Besançon: Cêtre, 2006.

Wandel, Lee Palmer. *The Eucharist in the Reformation: Incarnation and Liturgy*. New York: Cambridge University Press, 2005.

Weber, Alison. *Teresa of Avila and the Rhetoric of Femininity*. Princeton, NJ: Princeton University Press, 1990.

Whitford, David, ed. *Reformation and Early Modern Europe: A Guide to Research*. Kirksville, MO: Truman State University Press, 2007.

Wiesner-Hanks, Merry E. *Women and Gender in Early Modern Europe*. 2nd ed. New York: Cambridge University Press, 2000.

Wiethaus, Ulrike. *Maps of Flesh and Light: The Religious Experience of Medieval Women Mystics*. Syracuse, NY: Syracuse University Press, 1993.

Wolfe, Michael. *Changing Identities in Early Modern France*. Durham, NC: Duke University Press, 1997.

About the Editors

KATHRYN A. EDWARDS received her PhD from the University of California, Berkeley. She is associate professor of history at the University of South Carolina. She is the author of *Families and Frontiers: Re-creating Communities and Boundaries in the Early Modern Burgundies* (2002) and editor of *Werewolves, Witches, and Wandering Spirits: Folklore and Traditional Belief in Early Modern Europe* (2002). Her current research focuses on early modern European beliefs about ghosts.

SUSIE SPEAKMAN SUTCH received her PhD from the University of California, Berkeley. She is a postdoctoral research fellow at Ghent University. Her research focuses on late fifteenth- and early sixteenth-century literature and civic culture in the southern Low Countries.